"I do believe something very magical can happen when you read a book. Richard's book is the magic that helped him achieve more than he could have ever dreamed! It is a must read wherever you are in your journey."

—*Melvin Brown II, Federal Government Senior Executive*

"Richard has done a remarkable job summarizing, in an actionable and practical format, what it really takes to advance your IT career. Having spent most of my career in the IT field, I can relate to and approve of the advice and I wish I had had this guide when I started my career in IT!"

—*Magnus Nylund, chief operating officer (COO)*
of Learning Tree International

"Richard Spires is an experienced and passionate leader. He believes in giving back and supporting the success of others. Through his book, he gives a gift to the IT community by providing a thoughtful and practical guide on being successful in IT. Thank you, Richard."

—*Renee P. Wynn, former CIO of NASA*

"Richard has distilled his experiences and lessons learned from an impressive career in Information Technology into concise recommendations that are both insightful and common sense. It is destined to become a must read for those embarking on their career in one of the IT disciplines."

—*Robert Shay, former partner at Ernst & Young and COO*
of Capgemini Government Solutions

Success
in the
Technology Field

A GUIDE FOR ADVANCING YOUR CAREER

Richard A. Spires

successinthetechnologyfield.com

BookLocker

BookLocker

BookLocker.com, Inc.
200 2nd Avenue South, #526
St. Petersburg, FL 33701

This book is available at a discount when purchased in quantity for an organization's internal use. For more information contact BookLocker.com, Inc. using the form contained at the link https://secure.booklocker.com/booklocker/wholesale/order.php.

Library of Congress Cataloging-in-Publication Data
Names: Spires, Richard A., author.
Title: Success in the Technology Field – A Guide for Advancing Your Career /
Richard A. Spires / First Edition.
Identifiers: LCCN 2021906908
ISBN 978-1-64719-546-5 (Hardcover)
ISBN 978-1-64719-547-2 (Paperback)
ISBN 978-1-64719-548-9 (Epub)
ISBN 978-1-64719-549-6 (Mobi)
Subjects: BISAC
SEL027000 Self-Help/Personal Growth/Success
BUS107000 Business & Economics/Personal Success
TEC000000 Technology & Engineering/General
COM000000 Computers/General

Book design by Rob Hudgins & 5050Design.com

Printed on acid-free paper.

*To all the mentors who have supported me
throughout my career*

Table of Contents

Foreword

In 2013, I had the honor of presenting the Federal Computer Week Fed 100 Government Eagle Award to Richard Spires. The Eagle Award is a pinnacle achievement recognizing outstanding contributions to the field of federal information technology. It was a well-deserved recognition of Richard's outstanding government leadership, first as chief information officer (CIO) of the Internal Revenue Service (IRS), then as CIO at the Department of Homeland Security (DHS). I chose as my theme for the award presentation that Richard was the epitome of "cool" in his role as a technology leader. I noted that I had worked with a number of outstanding technology executives over my career, but I had never run across anyone who was more calm and collected, more unflappable, more the emulation of that analogy about the duck that looks so calm on the surface of the pond while both paddling furiously under the water and simultaneously letting the rain just wash right off its back. I even went so far as saying that if that year's winner was holding a martini, shaken not stirred, we might just confuse him in his tux with ... Bond ... James Bond.

Granted, it was a light-hearted way to keep the attention of a thousand black-tie-garbed industry and government leaders, but I did mean every word. Richard is extremely cool under fire.

I have had the honor of knowing Richard for many years, and he has consistently gone above and beyond throughout his technology career in both industry and government. Faced with some of the largest cultural change challenges in the federal government, he drove a number of outstanding accomplishments both at DHS and IRS. But his leadership went far beyond just impacting two very large federal agencies. In his leadership of the Federal CIO Council, he successfully championed cross-government initiatives, mentored federal leaders, and fostered the crucial dialogue between industry and government to work together to get the mission accomplished.

And bookending his federal career, he has also been an outstanding private sector executive, delivering results, driving business value, and demonstrating thought leadership.

As I noted that spring night in 2013, he doesn't just get the job done; he gets it done while simultaneously bringing the rest of the technology community along with him. He is a true believer that a "high tide raises all boats." And, nowhere is that more evident than in the passion and commitment he has demonstrated in both leading and mentoring numerous up-and-coming technology executives.

Technology is a fascinating field of endeavor. The pace of technology change is swift, the stakes high, and the opportunities tremendous. And, it's a career field where success comes from being more than just a technical expert; it demands incredible change management, business acumen, and leadership skills. No one knows that better than Richard.

In this book, you will find a roadmap that will help ensure both your success and your satisfaction with your career choice. And it's a road that Richard has successfully walked; his stories and anecdotes are well-lived and well-told. You'll never meet a technology leader of greater integrity and compassion than Richard, he has truly been the embodiment of the twelve recommendations that he offers within these pages. And his commitment to giving to others has been a hallmark of a truly successful life and career.

Enjoy his book; I know I did. Then, inspired by his insights, pick up the brush and paint an even brighter future. And remember to pass along your wisdom and life lessons to those who come after you. Technology is, like leadership, all about people, and definitely a team sport!

David M. Wennergren
CEO, American Council for Technology – Industry Advisory Council (ACT-IAC)
Chair and Fellow, National Academy of Public Administration (NAPA)
Former CIO, U.S. Department of the Navy
Former Vice Chair, U.S. Federal CIO Council
Former Managing Director, Deloitte Consulting LLP

Preface

In 2018, the CompTIA Partner Summit organizers invited me to present at their upcoming conference. But they were looking for something different—a showcase presentation not focused on a specific technology. So, we tossed around some ideas. The organizers were intrigued by my career and the leadership roles I had held, so we agreed I would address what it takes to succeed in a career in technology. That was the first time I organized my thoughts about the lessons I have learned in my career and how they might help others. The presentation was well-received, with several people thanking me for my candor and for providing them with practical advice based on my experiences. Subsequently, I refined and repeated the presentation at two other conferences, including a large Microsoft government conference. And I started to think about capturing the lessons and recommendations in a book.

I have read numerous self-help books, some on improving one's personal life and some related to achieving greater business success. These books typically appeal to individuals across a broad spectrum of backgrounds and professional interests. While undoubtedly useful, such books necessarily shy away from over-emphasizing a particular industry. I have typically found such books wanting, particularly in terms of the actions someone seeking success should take and the behaviors that will improve the probability of becoming successful in a chosen career discipline.

Related to the technology field, and in particular information technology and cybersecurity, there are countless books, textbooks, articles, and training courses that cover all manner of technical disciplines. Whether it is technical theory, practical application of a particular technology, or the process and management disciplines needed to implement and operate technology effectively, there is available material across all technical and process disciplines. Yet, when it comes to how a technologist or someone choosing to work in the technology field plans and advances a career, surprisingly little material exists.

Every individual is unique, and how someone defines success in their career will differ markedly from others. Not everyone in the technology field wants to be a chief information officer (CIO) or chief executive officer (CEO). Some individuals wish to lead in other ways, as vital individual contributors, perhaps by developing specialized expertise in a technology or process discipline. Career planning and taking steps to advance a career is a personal endeavor. Everyone needs to chart their own path, defining their own career goals.

Yet, within the technology field, there are critical areas of knowledge, skills, and behaviors that, if pursued and adopted, provide a significantly improved chance of career advancement, irrespective of how one defines career success. I have learned lessons through my journey, both based on my own experiences and by observing many others in our technology field. I believe some of these lessons are universal to everyone in technology-related disciplines, whether someone is a software developer, a project manager, or a salesperson for a corporation offering technology-based solutions. So, I decided to write this book with the hope that you, as a reader, will gain insights from my experiences and lessons.

What makes me credible—why should you take the time to read this book and potentially embrace its recommendations? I have had the privilege of working in the information technology and cybersecurity fields for more than thirty-five years. Starting as an entry-level engineer and moving into IT project management, I eventually rose to become the program manager of one of the largest IT modernization programs ever undertaken. From there, I served as CIO at two of the largest federal government agencies. I recently served as the CEO of one of the world's largest and best-known technology training and workforce development corporations. And I have been involved with and invested in a number of technology-based start-ups—three of which have yielded substantial financial returns for their investors. Along the way, I have received numerous awards, and I am particularly proud of having been recognized by my alma maters. I was named a Distinguished Alumnus of the University of Cincinnati's College of Engineering in 2006 and inducted into the George Washington University Engineering Hall of Fame in 2019.

In structuring this book, I present twelve recommendations. Some of the recommendations involve adopting crucial behaviors that apply throughout one's career, while others are actions one should take, some more relevant early in one's career, and others more relevant later in one's career. Through this structure, I hope you can use these recommendations as a career planning aid, supporting you in developing new skills and abilities and adopting the behaviors needed for success. The book's last recommendation is to "Give Back," in which you work to support the next generation of leaders in your field. This book is one way in which I am working to give back. I sincerely hope you get meaningful insights from this book—insights that will help you, whether starting your career right out of school, hoping to land your first management job, or looking to advance as a seasoned executive or technologist.

Richard Spires
March 2021

Chapter 1:

A Career in the Technology Field – Defining Your Success

"There is no passion to be found in playing small—in settling for a life that is less than you are capable of living."

Nelson Mandela

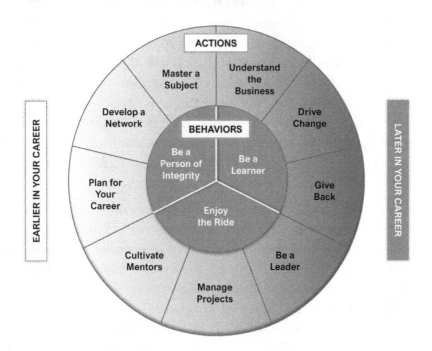

W hen we think of someone as being successful in technology, we often think of someone in a chief information officer (CIO) or chief information security officer (CISO) position. Or, for someone working in a company providing technology services or products, success is being a senior partner in a technical professional services organization or even the chief executive officer (CEO) of a product corporation. Undoubtedly, such individuals are successful, having earned such positions through years of hard work and dedication to developing the required skills and abilities for such positions.

Yet, some of the most successful individuals in the technology field never manage others. Some are competent technologists who advance the state of a particular technology or develop system architectures to address exceptionally complex business requirements. And they love the work they do. And others, in sales or business development roles, thrive on finding the match between their corporation's product offerings and appropriate customers, working to ensure the customer derives significant value through the implementation and use of a particular technology-based solution. Individuals in these roles (and others) can be very successful. In technology-related disciplines, there are so many varied pathways to success. What constitutes success in your career—your career goal or goals—is ultimately your decision. You can get advice from others, from mentors, but only you know what inspires you—your passion.

Whatever are your career goals, there are numerous resources, including books and training courses, to support you. For instance, there are many books and courses on leadership and management. Likewise, there are resources available on all facets of technology to help those looking to improve their knowledge and technical skills. There are books and courses for sales professionals and business developers that will train you to sell, from understanding the value proposition to effectively dealing with and building relationships with buyers.

Interestingly, however, few books address how to succeed in technology-related disciplines, cutting across all the roles, from executive to manager to self-contributor. It seems that some authors and publishers shy away from a broad-based approach because they feel the roles are too diverse in that the skills, abilities, and behaviors needed by a technologist are so different from a manager. They suppose there is little value in emphasizing the commonality and providing insight that can support everyone who works in technology or has a job substantially related to technology. But in my more than thirty-five years of work experience, starting as a technologist and individual contributor and rising to become a CIO and CEO, I have seen skills, experiences, and behaviors that are valuable to all, irrespective of one's current role and aspirations. This book explores those skills, experiences, and behaviors. Based on my own lessons learned and what I've gleaned by observing many successful individuals throughout my career, I've developed twelve recommendations designed to support your career in the technology field, providing advice to help you achieve your goals.

The Twelve Recommendations

Of the twelve recommendations to support those working in a technology-related field, three address your behaviors. These recommendations address how you handle and react in situations. Ideally, adopting these behaviors should be a focus from day one of your career. And these behaviors form the foundation upon which to build a successful career, as well as helping to support you in your personal life.

The other nine recommendations are specific actions for you to take. Overall, these actions develop knowledge, skills, and abilities (KSAs) in various subjects that support you in achieving your career goals. You should think of these recommendations in terms of their proper sequencing. Some of the recommendations are typically actions you will address early in your career, while others typically apply mid- or later in your career. Career paths vary greatly, so it is certainly possible that someone relatively early in their career may need to focus on recommendations labeled as "Later in Your Career." And it is undoubtedly the case that many of the recommendations labeled "Earlier in Your Career" are actions that you will want to sustain throughout your career.

The recommendations are grouped by career phases to help you visualize your career arc. While easy to understand as you read this book, twelve recommendations are impossible to address simultaneously. As you read, you should be thinking about your career plan over a twenty-to-thirty-year span, but with a focus on actions to take in the next five years. Especially if you are starting or are early in your career, the focus must be on the foundational behaviors and earlier-in-your career actions. These are building blocks for long-term success. Remember that your plan is your own, and there is no optimal plan. But you need to be realistic, as mastery of some of these recommendations is not just about taking a course and gaining a certification. It is about gaining an in-depth understanding of a subject and obtaining work experience over the years, so you are competent in a subject, enabling you to deliver value for your organization.

And adequately planning for your career is not just about obtaining specific technical knowledge and skills, it is also about addressing people-related skills, such as collaboration, management, and leadership, that so many of us technologists undervalue. Interestingly, in Learning and Development circles, sometimes these skills of dealing with other people are labeled "power skills" to showcase their critical importance to both an individual's and an organization's overall success.

The following figure depicts the twelve recommendations, grouped by behaviors and actions, displaying the sequencing from earlier to later in your career.

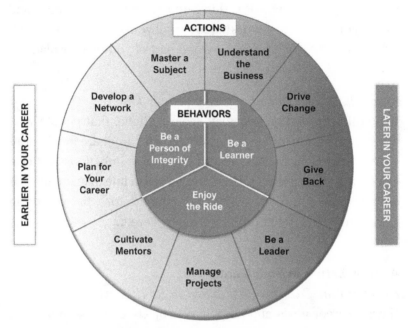

Twelve Recommendations for Professionals in the Technology Field

Below is a synopsis of the twelve recommendations. Each recommendation will be explored in-depth in later chapters.

Behaviors

Be a Person of Integrity – There is Nothing More Important

Are you a person of your word? Are you trusted and respected? If you want long-term success, this is mandatory. Every meaningful action you take and promise you make forges your reputation. If you lack integrity, you will not go far in the technology field, in which there are no short-cuts to success, and anything but truth will be exposed eventually.

Be a Learner – The Rate of Change Keeps Accelerating
One of the great aspects of the technology field is change—what we have available in the palm of our hand today was science fiction twenty years ago! But this rate of change is daunting and forces you to continue working to reskill yourself. It must be considered part of any job you have and part of your career plan.

Enjoy the Ride – Make It a Career, Not a Job
It is still valid, although it may seem a cliché, that people who develop a passion for what they do in their career are much more likely to enjoy sustained success. Passion is infectious and crucial to becoming a leader, whether you are in line management or an individual contributor. So have a passion for what you do in your career, and if you can't, find a new career.

Actions Earlier in Your Career
Plan for Your Career – Be Flexible in Its Execution
Having career goals and associated objectives is essential. You should have a written plan that lays out ultimate career goals along with objectives you wish to meet five, ten, fifteen, and twenty years out. And you should revisit and update your plan every year. Yet you should also be open to opportunities, ones that, in the short term, may significantly alter your plan. Seizing such an opportunity may end up being the best decision of your career.

Develop a Network – A Professional Network
Many of us in technology-related disciplines find developing relationships difficult. Yet business is and will always be a people-oriented endeavor. Working to develop and cultivate your professional network will pay you dividends for decades to come.

Cultivate Mentors – We All Need Them

We can't understand and address our professional weaknesses fully by ourselves. We need help from others. So, as you develop your network, be on the lookout for possible mentors, those who bring different perspectives and are not shy about providing you constructive feedback.

Master a Subject – Be Considered an Expert

The technology field is vast, with many subject areas. It helps if you, particularly earlier in your career, master a subject—to legitimately claim you are an expert in an area of technology or related process discipline. Not only does this burnish your reputation, it also provides perspective on what developing such expertise takes and means—knowledge that is valuable for managers and leaders.

Manage Projects – Understand How to Implement Technology

Whether a corporation, government agency, or non-profit, an organization enhances its capabilities to deliver and better serve its customers or constituents by successfully delivering projects and programs. Organizations might not always call them projects, but all the elements of good project management are needed to ensure the highest probability for success when implementing any significant operational change. Therefore, those in the technology field should learn how and gain experience managing projects.

Actions Later in Your Career

Understand the Business – Apply Technology to Create Value

Some of the most valuable people in any organization today effectively apply technology-based solutions to address business challenges. As one working in technology, how do you maximize your value? You should understand the business you support, the customers or constituents it serves, the value it provides, and the challenges it currently faces. In doing that, you significantly increase the chance you can bring to the table innovative, yet practical, technology-based solutions that can make a meaningful difference to your organization.

Be a Leader – Work at It

There are, of course, natural-born leaders, but for many of us technologists, people leadership does not come naturally. But that does not mean you cannot be a leader. It requires work, both in learning how to lead and in continuously practicing and improving your abilities.

Drive Change – Start on the Inside

Driving meaningful change in an organization is one of the more challenging assignments you can undertake. As such, it offers significant value potential for the organization and great potential for your career. Yet, there is considerable downside risk. Understanding the risk and making an informed decision on whether to step into a change agent position is crucial.

Give Back – Help the Next Generation

Helping others grow, being a mentor, seeing others succeed—as you advance in your career, these opportunities to support and mentor others become more frequent. By all means, take advantage of these opportunities, for you will not only help others, you will also learn and grow from such experiences. And you will continue to expand and enrich your network.

Using This Book

This book is not a replacement for other resources (including books, training courses, or work assignments) to develop your skills, abilities, and behaviors. **Think of this book as a companion to other resources, a guide regarding "what" to do to hasten your success in the technology field. Other resources provide you detailed information about "how" to go about it.** For instance, one of the book's recommendations is that technologists learn how to manage projects. Project management is a mature discipline with numerous resources that can support your learning. With proper training, augmented with the right kind of work experiences, you should be able to, within a five-year timeframe, develop the ability to manage technology-based projects effectively. This book offers you advice on what to do to achieve project management competence—other resources can provide you the specifics on "how" you manage projects.

The twelve recommendations are tangible, with specific items you can immediately include in your career plan. As an example—a theme that weaves through this book is self-awareness. We all have strengths and weaknesses, and understanding them and addressing your weaknesses can have a profoundly positive impact on your career and personal life as well. But how do you become more self-aware, then act on that awareness? Many people struggle to be true to themselves, not recognizing weaknesses that hold them back from the progress they should be making in their careers. The recommendations do address self-awareness, but indirectly. Creating a robust network and cultivating the right mentors provide you tangible, external mechanisms to gain the self-awareness everyone should have.

Another theme that weaves through the book is persistence. It is easy to state "have persistence" as a recommendation. But does it make sense to have persistence if the actual probability of you being successful in an endeavor is exceptionally low? And can you persist in the work if you have no passion for what you are doing? Once you align your innate capabilities (what you are good at) with work you enjoy doing and that gives you satisfaction, you will find your passion. And in doing so, you will undoubtedly have the persistence to guide yourself to success. The recommendations on developing a career plan, cultivating mentors, and enjoying the ride are meant to put you in the best position to find that alignment.

Each of these recommendations, by itself, can be of value to you in your career. **It is planning for your career (covered in Chapter 5), together with the other recommendations working in combination, that provide synergy for advancement and ultimate success.** So have that mindset. What recommendations logically group for you to improve your skills and abilities, advancing you towards what you define as success? Capture those groupings in a career plan with tangible milestones regarding actions you should take. And hold yourself accountable for their execution.

Time is a critical element to consider in your career planning. Early in a career, we tend to be in a hurry, which is an admirable trait. But so is patience. Recognize that most of these recommendations take years to "master," if that is even the right term. I continue to work on these recommendations myself, thirty-five years into my career. Think of time, from a career perspective, in five-year increments. If you set your mind to it and persist, you can "master" a recommendation in five years. For instance, you can become an expert in a subject in five years—not easy, but possible. And if you do that, think about the progress you will have made in such a short time!

Lastly, use this book as a reference when reviewing your career progress and plans. You should make it a yearly habit to review your career plan. Further, recognize and accept that we all experience hardships and failures in our careers. Plans rarely turn out exactly as initially conceived, and you will experience setbacks that will result in missed milestones in your career plan. Have patience at these times. But when you are at a cross point or feeling a bit unmoored, refer back to this book and its recommendations to recalibrate your focus on your career. Are there steps you should take to address gaps in knowledge, skills, or abilities? Do you need more hands-on experience in a particular technology or discipline? Are there recommendations in this book that you now need to address? Revise your plan as appropriate, learning from the current setback.

Conclusion

Here are a few last thoughts as you move into the heart of this book. As described at the beginning of this chapter, your career is your journey. No one else can pinpoint your destination nor determine the right steps for you. My approach to supporting you is to relate key events in my journey and those of others, noting what I learned from them, and how that crystalized into the twelve recommendations provided in this book. These recommendations don't define your success or journey, but they help you determine what success looks like for you in the technology field and what steps you should take on your journey.

Key Takeaways from Chapter 1:
A Career in the Technology Field

- In the technology field, there are so many varied pathways to success. Your career is your journey, and only you can determine what career success means to you.
- This book provides twelve recommendations to support your career in the technology field, whatever you aspire to achieve.
- The twelve recommendations consist of three behaviors and nine actions. The recommendations are:

Behaviors

> Be a Person of Integrity – There is Nothing More Important
> Be a Learner – The Rate of Change Keeps Accelerating
> Enjoy the Ride – Make it a Career, Not a Job

Actions Earlier in Your Career

> Plan for Your Career – Be Flexible in Its Execution
> Develop a Network – A Professional Network
> Cultivate Mentors – We All Need Them
> Master a Subject – Be Considered an Expert
> Manage Projects – Understand How to Implement Technology

Actions Later in Your Career

> Understand the Business – Apply Technology to Create Value
> Be a Leader – Work at It
> Drive Change – Start on the Inside
> Give Back – Help the Next Generation.

- Think of this book as a companion to other resources, a guide regarding "what" to do to hasten your success in the technology field. Other resources provide you details of "how" to go about it.
- It is the planning for your career, combined with the other recommendations, that provide synergy for advancement and ultimate success.

This book's recommendations help you determine what success looks like for you in the technology field and what steps you should take on your journey.

Behaviors

Chapter 2:

Be a Person of Integrity – There is Nothing More Important

"Integrity is one of several paths—it distinguishes itself from the others because it is the right path... and the only one upon which you will never get lost."

M.H. McKee

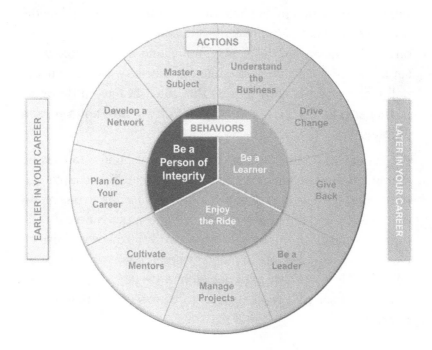

We are living through some trying times. Here, in the United States, we are a nation divided, with more coarseness, less civility, and less honesty in our politics than we have ever seen in our lifetimes. So many Americans seem to accept outright lying by many politicians. In reality, many silently disapprove. However, our politics have become so polarized that many Americans bite their tongue, still approving of their candidate despite the behavior. One might be thinking that such behaviors, the lying, the hypocrisy, the failure to keep promises, are becoming normalized in our society.

Yet as the title of this chapter states, there is nothing more important in your career than being a person of integrity. But this rule goes even further. In my definition of success, earning rewards with talent, hard work, and persistence is the essence of success. I would not view myself as professionally successful, despite the positions I held or the amount of money I made, if I knew I did not earn my achievements honestly. Now, someone else's values can differ from mine, and many people don't set a very high bar when it comes to morality, as our current political climate is showing us. But you will have little or no lasting success in the technology field if you are not a person of integrity.

Integrity is defined as the quality of being honest and having strong moral principles, being morally upright. This chapter explores the two concepts of being honest and having strong moral principles. Undoubtedly, if you are dishonest, that automatically calls into question your morality. But having strong moral principles is more complex and nuanced when it comes to someone's behavior. Here is where hard decisions arise in your career—decisions that set your reputation as to whether you are a person of integrity.

Honesty

Our field delivers value to others through the use of technology. In terms of products and services offered, it is an exacting field. Many other industries' products and services are influenced more by human tastes and preferences. That is less so in many technology-based services and products, because they perform certain defined and documented functions. One can factually determine whether such a product or service delivers such functions correctly. It is like the difference between what is known as hard and soft sciences. For instance, mathematics is a hard science, in that there are unchanging truths (fundamental theorems) that underpin mathematics, and humans and our actions or feelings do not influence these truths. Soft sciences, such as economics or psychology, are focused on how we can better understand human behaviors in our world. There are few, if any, unchanging truths in the soft sciences, and they evolve as we learn more about ourselves and how we act, as individuals and in groups.

The analogy is not perfect, as indeed all business, including the technology field, involves humans' interactions. Yet, there is just no short-cut to developing and delivering technology-based solutions and services. If you can't deliver what you promised, the truth is easily exposed, making it difficult to bend reality. The culture in our industry is like a hard science—it is one of exactness and representation of the facts as they exist, not as we might like them to be. Significant value is placed on presenting the facts correctly, whether those facts are positive or negative. In other words, ours is a culture that values, and even demands, honesty. It is ingrained in many of us in the field, and we take affront with those not living up to the standard.

During my thirty-five-year career in technology, I have encountered particular individuals who were dishonest. And I am not just referring to someone telling a "white lie" or an exaggeration that has little or no real impact. I am referring to dishonesty that has significant business consequences. I have seen status reports that contained falsehoods regarding the actual state of a project, downplaying or not even acknowledging serious performance issues. I have been lied to directly by executives during intense negotiations in which they were attempting to gain an advantage on a particular issue. I have seen other executives lie in attempts to cover their failings.

In such situations, it damaged the career of the individual being dishonest. Some of them lost their jobs, and even if they were allowed to stay, it damaged their reputation. There is a stigma in our industry attached to those that are dishonest, and it is difficult to recover a tarnished reputation.

In regard to honesty, when it comes to your professional career, be truthful in all of your dealings. At times, that may not be easy, as there are circumstances when you may wish to bend the truth. You may rationalize, telling yourself this one lie is the right approach, as you may avert immediate criticism of yourself and perhaps your organization. And you might think that the truth will not come out. Or maybe you have a plan to urgently address the issue causing you to lie. Be careful not to fall for these specious arguments. The chances someone will expose the lie are relatively high. **Be willing to take the heat—tell the truth even when it is difficult to do so.** Sure, it is difficult at that moment, but the price you will pay is much less than what it will cost you when you lie, and that lie is then exposed.

There is one last point on honesty. If you make a promise or give your word, then you must fulfill that promise. Anything less than that is being dishonest with yourself and others. If a situation arises and you cannot keep a promise, immediately let the other person know and explain why you cannot keep your promise. And, if need be, make amends. Not keeping promises will tarnish your reputation. So take care when making a promise, no matter how small or seemingly insignificant.

Moral Principles

The case for being honest in your professional dealings is straightforward. But business is about human relationships, and there is always complexity. In your career, you will undoubtedly find yourself in situations that make you uneasy when someone asks you to do something that does not feel right. It harkens to another quote from M.H. McKee:

"Wisdom is knowing the right path to take. Integrity is taking it."

Humans have moral compasses and, most often, we know what the right path is. However, many times it can be challenging to choose that path.

There have been instances in which I found myself faced with moral dilemmas in my career. I am providing a few personal examples below, along with an example from a mentor. My intention is not to criticize or demean others, but to provide insight and lessons that came out of struggles with moral situations. I am not providing any individual's name, title, or even an organization name in these examples.

Early in my career, I was involved in a network-design project in which I had a leading technical role. Near the project's completion, as we were preparing the final report, I discovered an error in the analysis. The error was the result of a miscommunication between another project team member and me. Correcting the error would take some significant rework, delaying the final report's delivery by a week or two. Yet, the error was relatively minor, and I knew correcting the error would have little to no impact on the report's recommendations. I agonized as to whether to let it go and not report it to the project manager. But I knew it was wrong not to report the error. We ended up redoing the analysis to correct the error and delivering the report late to the client. I took heat—rightfully—for not doing the proper quality review earlier in the project, but I was relieved, knowing that I had done the right thing.

One of my mentors related a story about being a person of integrity. He was a newly installed manager, and he had a moral challenge to address—six of his direct reports were under-qualified, underperforming, and overpaid. What to do in such a situation? Terminating them immediately would, in the short term, be considered the proper thing to do. But did he owe these direct reports something more? With approval from his supervisor, he met with each one individually, offering them the option of undergoing aggressive upskilling (at the company's expense) or taking the time they needed to find another opportunity elsewhere. In each case, because of an honest appraisal and recognition of a moral obligation, each landed in a more satisfying and secure career. It also made my mentor more confident as a leader and at peace with his conscience.

As a third example, I worked for a boss who had a very different set of values from mine. I did not care for how this individual treated employees, showing little professional respect, especially to support staff. But even more concerning was the individual's willingness to make promises to customers that I knew would be difficult for our organization to deliver successfully. Not impossible, so I could not state this individual was being outright dishonest, but rather putting the organization at risk. As the quote above states, the more I worked with this individual, the more convinced I was that we were not on the right path. I struggled with this for several months and had a couple of direct conversations with the individual to better understand the rationale for their actions. But my unease continued to grow. Ultimately, it led to a split, in which both of us agreed it was best I leave the organization. I felt I was compromising myself and my integrity, even though it was not my actions that were causing my unease.

As a final example, an employee who was a direct report to me was brilliant and, as an individual contributor, very valuable to the organization. But this employee was also disruptive to the organization, not working well as a team member, and not treating peers with the respect I like to see in the workplace. I have faced this type of situation a few times in my career. It can be difficult for a manager to decide if such an employee is worth keeping, balancing the individual's value versus the disruption to the organization.

But in this particular instance, another employee came to me complaining of how this first employee was behaving, not in keeping with what I consider to be professional behavior in the workplace. The second employee was not lodging a formal complaint, but it was also clear that this employee felt that I should address the first employee's behavior. After conferring with our human resource specialists, I counseled the first employee, yet the conduct improved only slightly. Then the first employee started making accusations against other employees. I ended up letting the first employee go, even though the employee was quite valuable. I based my rationale partly on the first employee's treatment of others. But my decision also involved the willingness of the first employee to make unfounded accusations regarding others' behaviors. Such accusations, as our human resources organization investigation proved, had no basis in fact. The lack of integrity on the first employee's part led me to take action.

I gave up a lucrative position because I would not compromise my integrity. And I had to let a valuable employee go because the individual lacked integrity. For me, the decisions were challenging at the times, yet the path was clear, and I knew what was right. And as I look back on my career, I have always tried to be a person of integrity. That is so important to me, as it is an integral part of my success.

Often when dealing with issues related to integrity, understanding of what action to take is very clear. But as the above examples demonstrate, some situations will undoubtedly arise in your career that can be difficult and complex. And there can be near-term consequences regarding the actions you take, both for yourself and others. In such cases, first work to understand the facts. As a mentor once told me, "get the facts and validate them, or the facts will get you and bring you down." This is especially the case in dealing with tense or emotional situations. If you are addressing possibly improper employee behavior, leverage your human resources department to help you discover the facts, as I did in the last example. Once you have high confidence you fully understand the facts, put your moral compass to work. If you are still unsure what action to take, turn to a supervisor, mentor, or possibly a human resources specialist, if appropriate. But if the situation involves others, always ensure the privacy of everyone involved. Through this approach, you are gaining the wisdom to determine the right path. And once you know the right path— have the integrity to take it.

Conclusion

There are few guarantees in life—death and taxes, as the saying goes. **But it is a guarantee that you will set yourself apart from most people if you are a person of integrity.** While this is a pessimistic view of humanity, many people, when faced with choices regarding which path to take, will take the easy path. But that rarely is the right path, the path of integrity. So be honest and have strong moral principles. Be a person of integrity, someone whose word is their bond, and someone who will do the right thing, even in the face of adversity.

Key Takeaways from Chapter 2:
Be a Person of Integrity

- One might think that lying, hypocrisy, and the failure to keep promises are becoming normalized in our society.

- Yet you will have little or no lasting success in the technology field if you are not a person of integrity.

- Integrity is defined as the quality of being honest and having strong moral principles, being morally upright.

- There is a culture in the technology field, a culture born of the hard sciences. It is one of exactness and representation of the facts as they exist, not as we might like them to be. As such, there is a significant value placed on presenting the facts correctly, whether those facts are positive or negative. In other words, there is a culture that values, and even demands, honesty.

- Regarding honesty, the recommendation to you is simple. When it comes to your professional career, be truthful in all of your dealings. Be willing to take the heat—tell the truth even when it is difficult to do so. And be a person of your word, fulfilling your promises.

- Business is about human relationships, and there is always complexity. Humans have moral compasses, and most often, we know what the right path is. However, many times it can be challenging to choose that path.

- In dealing with people in tense and emotional situations, make sure you get the facts. If dealing with possible improper employee behavior, leverage your human resources department to help you discover the facts.

- You will set yourself apart from most people if you are a person of integrity. Too many people, when faced with having choices regarding which path to take, will take the easy path. But that often is not the right path, the path of integrity.

Be a person of integrity, as someone whose word is their bond, and as someone who will do the right thing, even in the face of adversity.

Chapter 3:

Be a Learner –
The Rate of Change
Keeps Accelerating

"One learns from books and example only that certain things can be done. Actual learning requires that you do those things."

Frank Herbert

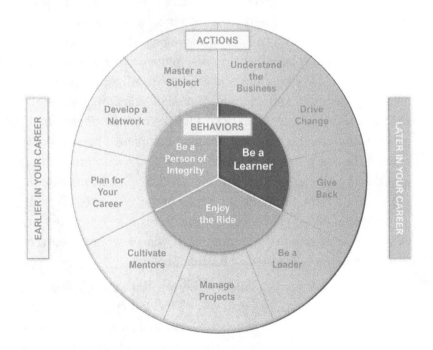

I t is a cliché to state that you need to be a life-long learner. But in the technology field it remains true. Technology evolves at a breakneck pace, with ever-more powerful computing, storage, and networking capabilities. Technology-based products rapidly avail themselves of these new capabilities, and the resulting product-launch cycle continues to shrink. When I graduated in 1984 and entered the workforce, hardware product major releases were typically three years apart. Today, major hardware releases generally are about a year apart. And with the advent of cloud computing and enhanced software development tools and techniques, the rate of change for software releases is every six to twelve months, with minor releases occurring every few weeks.

Soon after I joined Learning Tree International as CEO in late 2015, the company faced the reality of just how fast the industry was evolving. Learning Tree is a leading provider of technology training and workforce development services and, as such, it had developed and maintained its own courses that covered many facets of IT and related process disciplines. Our curriculum included training courses that covered most Microsoft products, including desktop applications, but also enterprise solutions such as SharePoint. Now Microsoft has its own product training courses, and most technology-training companies license those courses for their use in training others. Our value proposition was that being independent of Microsoft, we could provide insight into both the products' strengths and weaknesses. Typically, we would have our course authors provide one, or possibly two, major revisions to a course each year, keeping it current with Microsoft's latest release for that product.

But with the rise of cloud computing, this strategy was failing us. Microsoft's strategy is to rely on its cloud platform, Azure, and offer its software products on a usage-based rather than a license-based model. However, the issue for us was that once a software product was on a cloud platform, it becomes much easier to upgrade software products. Instead of a new release every six to twelve months, we found Microsoft putting out upgrades every two to four weeks. It quickly became impossible for Learning Tree to keep our courses up-to-date. So, within a few months of my joining Learning Tree, we decided to become a Microsoft Partner, enabling us to offer certified Microsoft courseware.

This story about Learning Tree highlights the accelerated change in technology and related products. Interestingly, this change does not apply just to technology products, but also to related process disciplines. Project management, as a discipline, is quite mature and, as such, relatively static. But process disciplines, such as Agile, DevOps, and now DevSecOps, continue to evolve rapidly. And this does not apply just to software engineering and development, but also other disciplines, such as systems engineering and data management. For example, there is a significant advancement in Model-Based Systems Engineering (MBSE) and related tools, such as SysML, to support the design and engineering of technology-based solutions to meet business requirements.

The ground under you is continuously in upheaval, no matter what you do in the technology field. In your career planning, you need to address this upheaval through continuous learning.

Education

The technology field is home to individuals of all types, from those with deep interest and background in a given technology, to those who enjoy implementing or administering solutions, to those who enjoy working to position the best solution to meet a customer's needs. There are particular knowledge, skills, and abilities (KSAs) that one needs to understand and master for each of these types of positions. The development of these KSAs starts in schooling as a child and continues as one enters formal schooling post-high school. Now, I have a bias for attaining a college education. Yet, the technology field has matured significantly, now encompassing many jobs that don't necessarily require a college education. For positions such as systems or network administrators, systems operations, and even some software development, vocational education options are available and flourishing.

The point is that, based on your career goals, you should first have a formal education that will provide you with the basic KSAs needed to meet those goals. And perhaps that does not require a college education, or maybe not a traditional four-year undergraduate degree. That is okay. If your career goals change later, you can evolve your career plan to add more formal education when needed. Still, education needs to be part of the planning early in your career and incorporated with specific educational objectives in an individual development plan (IDP). Chapter 5 provides more detail on career planning and the IDP.

Formal Learning

When I started my first job post-college (after obtaining a bachelor's degree), I also wanted to pursue a graduate education. I enrolled in a master's degree in electrical and computer engineering part-time and earned a degree in about three years. It was a good decision because there was direct benefit from some of the courses I took to the work I was doing in my full-time job. I was pleased to earn the degree, and it has been a help to me throughout my career.

But then I made a mistake. I failed to understand the importance of continuing to pursue additional formal learning through training. The company I was with at the time provided me excellent work experience. But the company was relatively small and had little in the way of help from a professional development standpoint. And none of my mentors pushed it. I did not fully understand the value that such formal training can provide until later in my career. Don't make that same mistake. Focus first on formal education, but then pivot to formal training and certifications to help you address the KSAs and behaviors you are looking to develop.

Having served as the CEO of Learning Tree International, I am a big proponent of formal training. But formal training is only one aspect of developing KSAs. Your IDP should have elements of formal training, self-study and research, on-the-job assignments to support skills and abilities development, along with mentoring. This multi-faceted approach can work quite effectively, particularly early in your career.

Today, there is a lot of course content in on-demand formats, meaning you can take a course by yourself, when you want, via the Internet. On-demand training can be especially valuable to cover foundational material in a subject. Taking training via an on-demand format requires significant dedication, and as such, completion rates of such courses can go below 20 percent. Augmenting on-demand training with instructor-led courses in a "blended learning" model has become prevalent and is considered best practice today. It can be particularly challenging to master advanced concepts with exclusively on-demand courses. The learner has no direct access to an instructor to ask questions and receive detailed answers and explanations. At some point in working on mastering complex subject material, the learner should have access to a subject-matter expert, typically an instructor, but at least a mentor.

Try to schedule formal training so you can immediately use your new skills in your job. So much is lost if you take a course and then can't apply any new skills or knowledge for months. By using the skills on the job soon after the training, you reinforce the learning and accelerate the movement to competence in a particular subject. And if you can interweave formal on-demand and classroom training with on-the-job experience, even better.

For example, if you are a software programmer and are learning a new software development language, take a course on that language's fundamentals. If you can then use the language over a couple of months on the job, you are now ready to take an advanced course on that language for a more in-depth treatment of specific facets of that language. And you may wish to augment the formal training with self-study on various advanced aspects of the language. Using all of these learning modes together is the ultimate form of "blended learning."

There are many different certifications learners can earn in various technology-related disciplines today, most of which are earned by completing one or more training courses and taking a proctored test to show a minimum level of knowledge. Indeed, you should investigate and set about earning certifications in your relevant subject as part of your IDP. But recognize that certifications, in and of themselves, do not convey practical expertise. An individual with a particular certification may still lack the complete set of KSAs to effectively fulfill a position's responsibilities. Most certifications are knowledge-based, but do not focus much on the practical use of skills and abilities.

Informal Learning

Once you have finished your formal education, there are few guidelines to support you in your career learning journey. Your employer may have requirements or expectations for additional learning that you must meet. And if you have earned professional certifications (for example, becoming a Project Management Professional (PMP)), they typically include requirements for continued learning over a specific timeframe. But realistically, you need to take your continued learning approach into your own hands. And this means addressing your approach to both formal and informal learning. In the realm of informal learning, undertake the following:

1. **Observe and ask experienced co-workers** – Focus on who already has expertise and experience in the subjects in which you wish to gain competence and even expertise. Refine the list of KSAs you are seeking for yourself by observing others. And even more importantly, discuss how they developed their expertise and how they keep current in their chosen subject area. What formal education and learning have they undertaken, and do they still engage in formal learning periodically? And what are their informal learning approaches for self-study and research? What trade periodicals do they read? Are there valuable Internet sites they use? What professional associations do they belong to? What conferences do they attend? All of this input can support you as you develop your IDP to address both your formal and informal learning approaches.

2. **Leverage your mentors** – Once you have mentors, use them to help you develop and refine your IDP for both formal and informal learning (Chapter 7 covers finding and cultivating mentors in detail). Based on your career goals, discuss what additional training, work assignments, and other experiences you should be pursuing to further develop your KSAs. A big part of informal learning is on-the-job experience. Probe your mentors for the types of work you should be seeking to gain valuable experiences. And keep your mentors abreast of your progress against your IDP. Share what you have learned and the changes you are contemplating. Solicit your mentors' feedback. This type of ongoing dialogue with a valuable mentor can provide you insights that you, by yourself, might take years or even decades to understand.

3. **Proactively seek knowledge and skill-building opportunities** – Routinely scan your selected subject areas for changes and emerging options that may affect your plans. A breakthrough in a particular technology, recent product an-

nouncement, or updated release of a new technical or process standard are opportunities for you to learn and develop additional skills. If you uncover a new development in one of the subjects you regard as significant and potentially valuable to you, obtain feedback from experienced co-workers and mentors. If you decide you need knowledge and skills for this new development, incorporate it into your IDP. Your career plans, and in particular, your IDP, should not be static. Given the pace of change, your IDP should evolve to support your formal and informal learning needs.

Ultimately, a great deal of informal learning is about your mindset. Do you have the "curiosity" to seek to understand as much as possible about a particular subject? The more passion you have about a subject, the more the hard work of becoming an expert becomes easier. If you are struggling with having that curiosity, it can indicate that you are in just a job and have not yet found your career passion. Continue to search for your passion as you continue learning, using your curiosity and what you enjoy as guides.

Conclusion

"Being a Learner" is such an essential trait that it is one of the three foundational behaviors you will need throughout your career. As you embark on your career, make it a point to continue formal learning beyond your education. Our field is moving so quickly, and there are always new technologies and processes to understand. Your professional value is highly dependent on maintaining your currency in your chosen subject and other related subject areas. You should have a career plan and related IDP with a tactical set of learning objectives to meet over the next five years. So, make formal and informal learning a planned habit, and you will be prepared for new opportunities when they arrive.

Key Takeaways from Chapter 3: Be a Learner

- It is a cliché to state that you need to be a life-long learner, but in the technology field, it remains true. Technology evolves at a breakneck pace, with ever-more powerful computing, storage, and networking capabilities.

- Rapid change does not just apply to technology and products but also related process disciplines. Project management, as a discipline, is quite mature and, as such, relatively static. But process disciplines, including Agile, DevOps, and now DevSecOps, continue to evolve rapidly.

- Whatever you do in the technology field, the ground under you is continuously in upheaval. In your career planning, you need to address this upheaval through continuous learning.

- There are particular knowledge, skills, and abilities (KSAs) that one needs to understand and master for each position in the technology field.

- Focus first on formal education, but then pivot to looking at which formal training and certifications can help you address the KSAs and behaviors you are looking to develop. But recognize that certifications, in and of themselves, do not convey practical expertise.

- Recognize the importance of informal learning, using both experienced co-workers and mentors to support you in developing plans for effective informal learning.

- Your individual development plan (IDP) should have elements of formal training, self-study and research, on-the-job assignments to support skills and abilities development, and mentoring. Use "blended learning," meaning using different training modes, to support developing mastery of a subject.

Your professional value is highly dependent on maintaining your currency in your chosen subject and other related subject areas. So make formal and informal learning a planned habit.

Chapter 4:

Enjoy the Ride – Make It a Career, Not a Job

"The only way to do great work is to love what you do. If you haven't found it yet, keep looking. Don't settle."

Steve Jobs

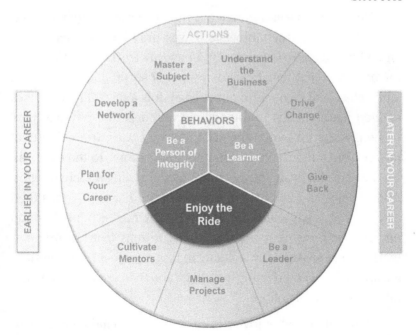

I f you are like many in the technology field, you spend much of your discretionary time working, and it is where you get much of your intellectual stimulation. As such, work should be something you enjoy doing, are good at, and get satisfaction from—it should become one of your passions. It isn't easy to get significant satisfaction from your work if it is a job rather than a career. A job is transient and meant to provide you a paycheck. A career, on the other hand, is something you do for your lifetime, and it should bring you much more than just monetary rewards. Indeed, many of us want a career where we achieve certain positions, financial independence, and even wealth. Yet other intangible rewards should go with a career, both in the personal satisfaction it brings and leaving the world better for our efforts. How you define success in your career is very personal, but you should include elements of service to others as part of that definition.

One intangible and significant career reward is enjoying your work. Like many technologists, I was drawn to science topics when I was a child. In particular, I have always been intrigued by the beauty of mathematics. So, it was not surprising that I would study electrical engineering in college. It is a discipline that uses applied mathematics to understand and describe physical phenomena across a wide range of important uses, from electrical power distribution, to wireless communications, to the electronics that are the basis for all computers and digital technologies. Additionally, as I will describe in detail in Chapter 8, I was then able to apply my passion for applied mathematics in my first job out of school, using mathematical algorithms in wide-area network design projects. I was lucky to find a subject I was passionate about that I could study in college and then apply it in my first job coming out of school.

Remember that enjoying your work goes hand-in-hand with being good at what you do. Early in your career, you might pick a particular subject because of your interest—you feel it is something you would enjoy doing. That's good, but if that subject requires innate capabilities that you lack, it will end in frustration and loss of that enjoyment. As described in Chapter 3, the technology field demands that you be a life-long learner, continually working on your KSAs in your particular subject. But to do that, you must have innate capabilities that underpin all learning in that subject—there is no way to compensate for a lack of innate talent. For example, I am tone deaf, having no ear for music. I enjoy the thought of being a professional musician, but no amount of tutoring or practice would ever get me to the proficiency to be a professional musician. And it would be a frustration even to attempt it.

Finally, you want to get satisfaction from your career. The importance of this was brought home to me when I first entered government in 2004, joining the IRS to take over the leadership of the Business Systems Modernization (BSM) program. Government employees take a lot of pride in what they do and, in particular, the agency in which they work. Even at the hated IRS, not only is there tremendous pride in the agency "funding America," but there is also a perverse sense of pride in being part of "one of the more hated institutions in America." There is a quote from Oliver Wendell Holmes Jr., "Taxes are the price we pay for civilized society." I love the eloquence and succinctness of the quote, and it is inscribed near the top of the IRS headquarters building at its main entrance on Constitution Avenue in Washington, D.C. The quote's placement is not too noticeable, but it did not take long in my tenure at the IRS for another employee to point it out to me. A small gesture, but it is a telltale mark of the pride the typical IRS employee feels for the institution.

I too came to appreciate that sense of mission and service in my years at the IRS and DHS. The time I spent in government service has been the most personally satisfying of my career. I loved the challenges we faced—technological, operational, and financial. And it meant so much to me to be part of something much larger than myself, something which can positively impact so many American lives. I never worked harder, and I could have made much more money at a private-sector corporation. Yet, I don't regret a day of my government service, and today, more than seven years after I left DHS, I still spend volunteer time supporting the improvement of federal government IT.

If you don't have passion for what you are doing professionally, recognize that not only is it reflecting on your happiness and well-being, but it is also evident to others. The challenge to you is to find something you enjoy doing, you are good at, and that gives you satisfaction. Those are the ingredients for finding your passion.

Changing a Career

It is a sad spectacle to see someone stuck in a career that makes them unhappy. Perhaps the individual is so risk-averse that they can't imagine a change, or they are close to retirement and just hanging on for monetary reasons. Whatever the issue, it is painful to see someone who does not enjoy what they are doing. And it is especially painful if the individual is in mid-career, with many years yet to work.

It is easy to advise that in such a situation, individuals should figure out what their passion is and pursue it. But for whatever reason, they struggle with such a significant change. Perhaps their financial position makes it difficult for them to make a change. Yet, one of the wonderful things about being in the technology field is the variety of career choices and the industry's continual evolution. If you are risk-averse, whatever the reason, there are steps to take if unfulfilled and unhappy in your career. Perhaps you can take classes in the evening to reskill yourself. Or you can tap your professional network to seek a mentor who can help you navigate such a change. Or you might even have the courage to approach your current employer and ask how to transition to a new position that will support you in achieving a new career path.

If you know you need to change your career, develop a multi-year transition plan. Give yourself a few years to develop new skills in your new chosen profession, while still ensuring you can pay the bills. Especially for the risk-averse, having such a plan will lighten your spirits as you embark on a journey that can give you what we all want—a sense of fulfillment in your professional life.

Staying In a Job

During your career, you will most likely have several positions in which you feel you have stalled. You are not growing your skills. The position is not what you expected. Or even worse, the environment is toxic, and it becomes ever more challenging to remain excited to stay in the position. Is there anything you can or should do to salvage the position? When do you pull the cord and exit? These can be difficult questions to answer.

I admit to being part of the older generation of workers in today's workforce. (I am at the tail-end of the Baby Boomer Generation, an age group that tended to stay in jobs longer than today's younger segment of the workforce.) Still, it is a red flag when I review a resume and see an individual who has held numerous positions and many of them with less than a two-year tenure. If these positions are in the same organization, that can indicate someone quite valuable—someone the organization is grooming for more senior roles. But it is the individuals who jump from organization to organization who concern me. If I hire someone in the technology field and they stay for less than two years that is a failed hire. Even if that individual is quite experienced, they can rarely step into a technology-related job and be highly productive in less than a year. So, the organization is getting little value from someone staying for less than two years.

In an earlier era (for example, when I came out of college in 1984), it was generally expected that new college grads would stay at a company for four or five years. And in my parent's generation, many professionals spent their whole career at the same company. But those days are gone. According to a survey from Express Employment Professionals, 71 percent of recent college grads stayed in their first job out of school for less than a year. So, changing jobs is not only more common—it is now more accepted. But is it necessarily better for the individual? Particularly in the technology field, it can take years for someone to become proficient in a position. So how much is a young person learning when they stay in a position less than a year? Undoubtedly, there are reasons that someone should move to a new position (and even a new organization). If they discover that the position will not advance them along their career path, they should move. Or if a new opportunity can accelerate them along their career path, then move. Or if the environment is so toxic that they cannot enjoy the job, then move. But if it is a move to make a bit more money, is that a good reason to move?

Early in your career, take the time to document a career plan. (The next chapter describes career planning in detail.) A plan that describes your long-term professional goals and short-er-term objectives will benefit you in decision-making over the next five years. Perhaps you have recently graduated with a technical degree (such as computer science or engineering). What would you like to be doing in five years? What are the skills and experiences you need to reach your five-year objectives? If you can do just this level of planning coming out of school, you can better assess your current position. Is the position enabling you to obtain skills and gain experiences to meet your five-year objectives? If not, then definitely go out and evaluate alternatives. But be realistic—recognize that all positions have their downsides and just because you have some frustrations in a position is not, in and of itself, a good reason to move. Also, recognize that with a position change (and in particular, an organizational change), there can be lost momentum in your professional development.

Similarly, in mid-career and later in your career, you should routinely analyze your current position. Given that you have significant work experience, you understand the frustrations with employment and are in a better position to gauge whether those frustrations rise to the level of forcing you to make a change. But having a five-year outlook and objectives continues to be valuable for you. Is your current job enabling you to develop the skills and gain experiences to support you in attaining your five-year objectives? If yes, then you are in the right position. And if a new intriguing opportunity does arise, assess whether this new opportunity enables you to either accelerate meeting your five-year objectives or significantly raise the probability of meeting those objectives. And evaluate whether this new position advances you to your ultimate career goals. Such decisions are some of the most important, and most difficult, in your career. Having a written career plan, with long-term goals and near-term objectives, gives you context to assess your choices.

Conclusion

You will have greater success in your career if you have a passion for the work. It shows in your outlook and ultimately in your job performance. There are such varying career paths in today's technology field that finding your passion should be achievable. So find your passion, develop a plan to pursue it, and execute the plan. This passion will enable you to have a career that can last a lifetime, bringing you much more than just monetary rewards. And once you have found your passion, you will begin to "enjoy the ride."

Key Takeaways from Chapter 4: Enjoy the Ride

- Work should be something you enjoy doing, are good at, and get satisfaction from—it should become one of your passions. It isn't easy to get much satisfaction if your work is a job rather than a career.

- Many of us want a career in which we achieve certain positions, gain financial independence, and even wealth. But there are intangible rewards that go with a career, both in the personal satisfaction it brings and leaving the world better for your efforts.

- If you don't have passion for what you are doing professionally, recognize that not only is it reflecting on your happiness and well-being, it is also evident to others. Seek your passion in your career.

- If you know you need to change your career, develop a multiyear transition plan. Give yourself a few years to develop new skills in your new chosen profession, while still ensuring you can pay the bills.

- During your career, you will most likely have several positions in which you feel you have stalled. You are not growing your skills. The position is not what you expected. Or even worse, the environment is toxic. If you are not advancing your career or the environment is so toxic you cannot enjoy the job, then move.

- Early in your career, take the time to document a career plan—such a plan includes your long-term career goals, along with five-year professional objectives. If you can do just this level of planning coming out of school, you can better assess whether you should stay in your current position.

- Even mid-career and later in your career, having a career plan that includes a five-year outlook and objectives provides you valuable context as you both assess your current position and assess new opportunities.

**Find your passion, develop a plan to pursue it,
and execute the plan. Once you find a passion,
you will begin to "enjoy the ride."**

Earlier in Your Career

Chapter 5:

Plan for Your Career – Be Flexible in Its Execution

"Our goals can only be reached through a vehicle of a plan, in which we must fervently believe, and upon which we must vigorously act. There is no other route to success."

Pablo Picasso

Few people in the technology field plan well before and during their careers. Frankly, no one taught us to do it. As children, many of us were attracted to science and were good at math in school. Or perhaps we were drawn to business and obtained an undergraduate degree in finance, accounting, or marketing. Or perhaps we earned degrees in liberal arts or general studies. Or we attended a vocational school. Coming out of school, we landed in work in the technology field because of the opportunities—it is such a growing field, with a need for technologists, but also professionals with many other skills, including analysts, accountants, sales, and marketing personnel.

For most young people, the high-school years are highly structured. Indeed, there are significant prerequisites to meet in school. And while there are electives, those are typically a smaller percentage of classes taken by a student. Even then, there are guidelines as to the types of electives required for graduation. Furthermore, most young people rely on parents or other caregivers to provide structure and advice during these formative years.

After high school, that structure typically continues. Whether someone is entering college, attending school to learn a trade, or joining the military, there are still significant prerequisites to be met. Then someone starts their career with their first job, and the structure that has propelled their professional and personal advancement is suddenly gone. For this reason, many companies, government agencies, and the military now offer structured onboarding programs for new employees and recruits. And many of these programs support new employees or recruits in developing more specialized skills for particular positions. That can be of value to both the employee and the company. But it is indeed the case that the company (or government agency) has as its priority developing skills that will support it in the near term. Many companies will profess they have development programs and are looking to hire candidates to develop over several years. And for so-called "rising stars," that is undoubtedly the case. But you should always understand that an employer is first looking out for its interests, not yours.

Another dynamic makes it even less likely that a company will serve to develop people early in their careers. As described in Chapter 4, most college grads will stay with their first employer for less than a year. So wittingly or not, most college grads take the reins of their careers soon after graduation. This, in and of itself, is not negative, as you should be the steward of your career. No one else dictates where your career should head or the next steps to meet your goals. That does not mean you should not rely on others for advice, but **ultimately you are in charge of where you want to end up in your career and the path you choose to get there.**

Develop a Plan

No matter where you are in your career, whether just entering the workforce or an executive with thirty years of experience, you should have a written career plan. This is especially important early in your career. I am not a psychologist, and I can't explain why, but I have found that if you take the time to think about and write down what you would like to ultimately accomplish in your career, you have a much better chance of achieving your goals. Both your conscious and subconscious minds work to achieve what you have planned, and this can work for goals that you have set that will take decades to achieve. Additionally, having a written plan makes it easy to review and test the validity of long-term goals and nearer-term objectives, as well as to evaluate your progress.

Remember that it is okay to be bold in your thinking. Let's say you have just earned your undergraduate degree and are starting your first job. Professionally, what would you like to be doing thirty years from now? Do you want to:

- Be running a company
- Be considered a world-renowned expert in an area of technology
- Be a tenured and respected professor at a major university
- Be a leading salesperson at a company with a hot technology?

Now someone coming out of school might say, "I don't know what I want to do even five years from now." But don't let that stop you in this exercise. You have things that excite you now. What are those? What do you want to get better at doing? What does that mean for a position you might hold thirty years from now? This exercise is so important because it gives you a long-term direction and focus. That, in turn, will drive near-term decisions that will move you toward that long-term goal. And it is okay if next year, or five years from now, or even twenty years from now, you change your mind. It is possible that what you end up wanting to do is entirely un-related to a goal you establish now, although that is unlikely. And, even so, driving success at any time during your career will open up opportunities you cannot currently fathom—that is a wonderful part of seeing someone grow and change over their career.

As you work on this exercise of establishing career goals up to thirty years in the future, take some time on the exercise. Ini-tially, write a list of all those things you most like to do in your work and play. Then make a separate list of all those things you feel you are good at (your innate capabilities). Now get both lists out and individually prioritize all your entries from first to last preference. Finally, lay the lists side-by-side and cross-evaluate them to correlate what you most like to do with what you are best at. The results will guide you in defining the range of career options. As you think about those career options, what would success look like for you? What goal would you like to achieve in each career option, and what would that mean in the position you would hold?

Then let it sit for a week and don't think about it. When you go back to the lists, your perspective might have changed. If you have some mentors, now is a time to solicit their feedback. Describe the exercise you are doing and go over your lists, career options, and potential goals with your mentors. What is their reaction? For each career option, can they see you in such a career meeting the goal you described? Do they feel you have the innate skills and temperament for such a career? Do they see in you a set of traits that would be ideal for a different career option and meeting a different goal?

Now give it another week and revisit your written career options and goals. You are likely to have some new thoughts that will refine your goals. You don't need to be overly precise. Suppose you want to be the CEO of a company thirty years from now. Perhaps you want to specify the type of company given your current interests, but don't focus at this time on the size of the company or whether it is public or private. As you move towards this goal and refine your plan, you will add more specificity.

Pick one professional position you wish to have that defines your primary goal—for example, being the CEO of an IT professional services company. That is to be your focus on your plan. You can then have one or two other goals, but they are secondary and support the primary goal. For instance, you may think you would enjoy teaching, so perhaps you would set a secondary goal of being a part-time adjunct professor teaching business or management.

Do not set two goals that reflect two different career paths, such as wanting to become the CEO of a company and wanting to be a tenured professor. Indeed, some have done both, but it is rare for someone to have the talents and discipline to accomplish both. Frankly, by setting two such goals, you will diffuse your efforts, decreasing your chances of achieving either. So set a primary goal, then set up to two other goals that, when executed, support you in achieving your primary goal.

While you should share these goals with your mentors to get career advice, do not share these goals with others. Your goals will not be appreciated or understood by many people. I remember once being a co-worker with a young man who was a couple of years out of school. He was self-assured and had big aspirations, which I admired. But one day, it got around the company that he had a custom license plate for his car with the license being "CEO 2 BE." Not the right decision on his part, and frankly, for almost all the other employees, that self-assuredness then came across as arrogance. Have big goals, but know with whom and when to share them.

Now that you have goals in a career plan documented, take three additional planning steps as shown in the figure and described below:

1. **Research and document the competencies required to meet your goals** – It is beneficial for you to understand the competencies needed to attain a goal. Competencies are the knowledge, skills, and abilities (KSAs), and behaviors required to successfully serve in a position that would mean you have attained your primary goal. For example, suppose you aspire to be a world-class technologist in a particular subject, perhaps an aspect of advanced software-defined networking (SDN). If you could wish yourself in that position today, what would that mean? What knowledge would you need in the field of networking, with particular emphasis on

SDN? What would you expect to be doing in the field as an expert? Would you be designing networks for clients, or perhaps advancing the capabilities of products in the field? As an expert, you would undoubtedly have to develop reports and make presentations of your work. All of these activities help define the skills and abilities necessary for the role. Finally, what about behaviors? Will you be in a management position? Do you want to serve as a leader in which you will inspire and motivate others? Or would you prefer to be in a position that requires significant collaboration to advance a product or technology?

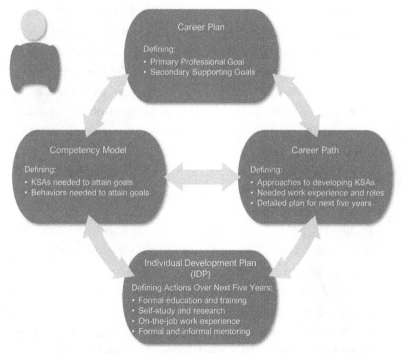

The Four Planning Steps to Develop a Comprehensive Career Plan

Research through reading articles and books regarding positions related to the goals you seek. It is usually not as simple as looking up a position's KSAs and expected behaviors.

Still, you can distill a position's competencies through studying books or articles, including biographies of those people who hold or have held such roles and their work products. Attend conferences related to your particular field of interest to learn what competencies are valued. Document these competencies in a concise, less than one-page competency model. Share this model with appropriate mentors to garner feedback and refine the competencies.

2. **Develop a career path plan that will result in you meeting your goals** – With defined career goals, and the competencies defined to meet them, you can identify a career path that will help you meet your goals. What are the experiences you need to develop the KSAs? What kinds of roles do you need to hold to gain those experiences? For example, suppose that you aspire to hold a CEO or chief operating officer (COO) position in a company. In that case, as you ascend in management positions, you should aspire to hold a position responsible for managing the organization that delivers the value to your customers, whether that be a product or service. Or if your primary goal is to be the top salesperson in a successful technology company, gaining experience in handling ever-larger accounts will be a vital set of experiences. Imagine a career path with actual roles and how long you will need to serve in those roles to truly master such a position. Gaining such mastery can rarely happen in two years. Think of five-year blocks as you do this exercise. Most importantly, set specific objectives you hope to accomplish during the next five years. What position do you expect to have five years from now, and what work experiences do you expect to gain during that time?

    This exercise does not lock you into any particular career path or the need to change jobs after five years. The objective is to understand the range of experiences you should be looking to gain over your career arc. As described below, how you get those experiences can differ markedly from any plan you develop, especially early in your career. But the act of researching and documenting a career plan in a few pages is well worth the time—it can be some of the most valuable time you will ever spend on your career.

3. **Develop an individual development plan (IDP)** – All of this planning provides you the information and context to develop your IDP. This five-year plan provides you with tangible actions to advance you along your career path so you can pursue long-term career goals. Based on your planned career arc and defining what you would expect to achieve over the next five years, the IDP describes the steps to take in the following areas:

- Formal education, such as working on an advanced degree

- Self-study and research, in which you remain current in subjects critical to your work and career goals

- Training and certification, which is becoming ever more crucial in technology-related disciplines

- Work experience to include specific roles you hope to hold over the next five years, the types of work you plan to do during that time to develop your KSAs, and actions to take that can address improving your behaviors to match your career goals

- Mentoring, both in terms of the types of new mentors you wish to cultivate and the benefits you hope to get out of having additional mentors.

Here is where mentors can be so helpful. When you share with a mentor a draft of your IDP along with your career goals and career path, they can help you refine your focus and prioritize your activities. You may have a tendency to take on more than you should, especially early in your career. Mentors can help you bring realism to your planning, and based on their knowledge of you, help you set the priorities for driving the most improvement to advance your career.

If you have never done this level of career planning, it can appear daunting. But the reality is that you should capture everything described above in no more than five pages. The research and interaction with mentors help you refine your long-term career goals and, in turn, result in near-term actions that can help advance your career. You should revisit these plans on an annual basis. Pick a time of year (say the beginning of the calendar year), and again go back and reflect on your career goals, refine your career path, and update your IDP based on any changes to your planned career path and what you were able to accomplish last year. And as described in Chapter 3, if at any time you decide you need new knowledge and skills development related to a subject of interest to you, incorporate it into your IDP. Given the pace of change in the technology field, your IDP should not be static, but evolve to support your formal and informal learning needs. This planning process, together with regular updates, will provide you lasting value through all stages of your career.

Be Flexible

Given the rigor I recommend in preparing and updating a career plan, you might have the impression that making a plan and not diverting from it is the best way to succeed. That is not the case. For example, when it came to my career, early on I had a primary goal of one day running an IT company, most likely a professional services company. Yet in mid-career I was offered an opportunity to come into government, at the IRS, to take over the then-struggling BSM program. While I had supported the government as a contractor, it was not originally an aspiration of mine to enter government, nor at the time did it appear that entering government would help me achieve my ultimate career goal.

Yet, upon reflection, the decision to enter the IRS and run the BSM program was the best career decision I ever made. Honestly, part of the reason I took the job was the sheer challenge of it. At the time, BSM was known as the largest and most complex IT modernization program ever undertaken. And the chance to lead the program and hopefully turn it around appealed to my desire to take on the hardest of jobs (this is a trait that I recognize has both positive and negative aspects). Furthermore, it was a high-profile position, which I thought could help me when I returned to the private sector. And lastly, I figured a few years in government would give me a perspective many private-sector executives serving government do not have—a chance to see how a government agency operates and manages its IT.

What I did not understand at the time was the intangible benefit of being part of something that helps all of society. As described in Chapter 4, it was a lesson for me when I first arrived at the IRS.

Interestingly, when I left government service the second time (after serving four years as the DHS CIO), I was asked to join the board of directors of Learning Tree International, one of the leading companies providing IT training and workforce development services. I would have never received such an invitation had I not had that government service. Furthermore, two years later, I was asked by the board of directors to step into the CEO role, a position I held for the next four-and-one-half years. And in taking on that CEO role, I met one of my career goals.

So, put in the rigor of making a career plan, especially identifying the KSAs and behaviors you will need for your long-term success. Develop an IDP and work diligently on it, so you are proud of the progress you have made when you look back in five years. But also **be open to new opportunities. Always meaningfully consider an opportunity that does not appear to line up with your career plan.** There are many ways to succeed, and sometimes an opportunity will arise that, once studied, is too good to pass up. That was certainly the case with me entering the government. By assessing the opportunity against my career plan, I realized it was an appropriate and elevating choice for me at that time. I had the KSAs to be successful in the position, and while it changed my career path, I did not change my career goals. In fact, I had confidence that by being successful in my government position, I would hasten my journey in achieving my career goals. Only you can assess opportunities as they come about, and if you keep an open mind, you too will be able to spot one that is too good to pass up.

There is one last point on being flexible. I have seen some extremely capable individuals who were, in my opinion, overly risk-averse. They had immense talents, but they became too comfortable in the same organization, or they felt like they could not take a financial risk a job change might entail. We all have different risk-tolerance levels, and in many ways, I would put myself on the conservative side of the mid-point. Yet, do not let risk overly impact your decisions, especially in early through mid-career. This is another benefit of doing career planning and keeping your plan current. If you have been with one organization for a long time (say more than six or seven years), be honest with yourself as to why you are still there. If you are advancing in your career as planned, developing the competencies in line with your plan, then stay. But if you are concerned about the risk of leaving, yet you are not meeting all the milestones you have in your career plan, consider making a change.

Conclusion

You will undoubtedly face significant setbacks and hardships in your career—even the most successful people have. During a challenging time professionally, it is not easy to keep your motivation up and drive yourself forward. Yet, a career plan with both long-term goals and short-term objectives that move you incrementally to your goals can be of value, especially during difficult times. These plans can help keep you motivated and help you recognize that perhaps part of the reason for your current difficulties are deficiencies you should address, probably in certain KSAs or behaviors. With your mentors' help, work to recognize what you can learn from your current situation and resolve to improve. Going a step further, revamp your IDP to directly address any deficiencies you have identified from your current difficulty. And be especially mindful to focus on developing skills and abilities that enhance your job performance, not just provide additional knowledge. A focus on your IDP is a means to accelerate your career.

Key Takeaways from Chapter 5: Plan for Your Career

- We work in the technology industry because of the opportunities—it is such a growing field, with a need for technologists, but also professionals with many other skills.

- No matter where you are in your career, you should have a written career plan.

- Have big goals, but know with whom and when to share them. Your goals will not be understood by many.

- Pick one major professional position you wish to have that defines your primary goal. You can then have one or two other goals, but they are secondary to that primary goal.

- In addition to your goals, your plan should include:

  1. **The competencies (KSAs and behaviors) required to meet your goals**

  2. **A career path plan that will result in you meeting your goals**

  3. **An individual development plan (IDP) that contains the specific actions you will take over the next five years to develop needed competencies.**

- Use your mentors to support you as you develop your career plan. Mentors can help you refine your focus and prioritize your activities.

- Revisit your career plan on an annual basis, updating your career goals, career path, and IDP.

- Be open to new opportunities. Sometimes an opportunity will arise that is too good to pass up.

**Ultimately, you are in charge of where
you want to end up in your career and the
path you choose to get there.**

Chapter 6:

Develop a Network – A Professional Network

"Networking is marketing. Marketing yourself, your uniqueness, what you stand for."

Christine Comaford

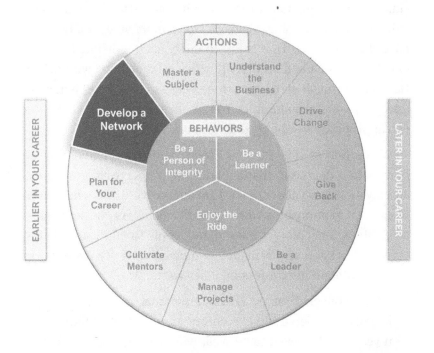

Business is about people and relationships. For most people, that is intuitive and requires little to no explanation. The opportunities you have in your career are, in no small way, dictated by the degree to which you build a professional network. This professional network represents the set of individuals you know and who know you in a business setting. But it is interesting to me that so many technologists don't grasp this concept. Many believe that good individual effort (and even brilliance) is enough. Too many technologists fail to spend sufficient time and effort building key relationships.

This book is for all who work in technology or technology-related fields. So that includes individuals of all backgrounds, skill sets, and personality types. But it is also true that many individuals in the technology field tend to be more analytically oriented and introverted. That is not to imply such individuals cannot have profound and incredibly positive relationships with others. But many struggle to develop the necessary skills and behaviors that support the building of robust professional networks that can appropriately support their careers.

I am one of those technologists, with two engineering degrees and a degree in mathematics. My father was an engineer and my mother an accountant. I am an introvert, and while I have wonderful relationships with my family members and some close friendships, I am slower than many people to cultivate relationships. It has been, and remains, significant work for me to develop and maintain my professional network.

After college, I joined SRA International, a highly successful technical professional services corporation. I stayed at SRA for sixteen years, and I was treated well, with some great work experiences that led to promotions up to the senior vice president level. Within SRA, I did work to establish relationships across the company. Likewise, I worked to build relationships with clients. Outside of working to build relationships within SRA and with my clients, I did little to enhance my network over the first sixteen years of my career. That was the biggest mistake I made during the early stage of my career. I believed that job performance was all-important. Therefore, I did not recognize the real importance of establishing a professional network and did not do nearly enough to cultivate such a network. And while I do not regret joining SRA—where I worked with many great people and gained important experience— this lack of networking put me in an awkward and disadvantaged position as I transitioned out of the company.

Building your professional network can be one of the most beneficial things you can do to succeed in your career. But it is also an endeavor that takes significant, sustained effort, and one with typically little direct payback early in your career. Yet it is also the case that if you make such an investment, it can benefit you ten or even twenty years later. In my case, I decided after leaving the IRS to do some consulting as a bridge to lining up my next full-time assignment. I was able to fairly rapidly obtain some clients, one of whom was a former SRA customer that I had supported many years prior. By then, this person was in a senior executive role in one of the country's largest professional service firms. It was a good fit because I supported activities this individual knew I had both the expertise and experience to perform well. This was a lesson for me in the importance of developing professional relationships.

Steps to Building Your Professional Network
In whatever stage of your career, it always makes sense to continue to invest in building and then maintaining your professional network. There are three key steps you should take in developing your professional network.

1. **Start with Your Organization** – Whatever type of organization you're in, get to know other employees throughout

your organization, emphasizing developing relationships with others working in technical or process disciplines that interest you. Showing curiosity in others' work and getting their advice is a sure way to open doors and begin to build relationships. Suppose you do stay in an organization for more than two years. In that case, you have a chance to potentially leverage those relationships directly as you look for work assignments that will enhance your knowledge and skills in support of your career plan. You want to be known as someone who sees assignments through to completion—your willingness to stick with a position in an organization for two years demonstrates your commitment.

If you work with customers or partners from other organizations, use those opportunities to enhance your network. Don't force it, but if you have a chance to work closely with customers, you not only increase your network, you gain valuable insights into how to act as a provider to customers and how to serve customers best in your chosen field.

2. **Find the Right Professional Association** – A critical way to rapidly build a meaningful professional network is to get involved in a professional association. Numerous professional associations in the technology field are aligned with a technology subject, process discipline, or industry. Associations are a meaningful way to broaden your network rapidly, well beyond your organization. But do your homework. You should pick an association that suits you and fits well with your career goals. And it should be one that fits your values. You should feel comfortable supporting the association's mission, and as you begin to interact with its members, you should feel an affinity with these people. They should not only be useful professional contacts, but people from whom you can learn.

Although it did not happen until mid-career, I became very involved with the American Council for Technology – Industry Advisory Council (ACT-IAC). This unique non-profit association has members from both government and industry and focuses on improving government through the proper leverage and management of technology. Within a couple of months of learning of ACT-IAC, I knew it fit my views regarding my passion for government IT. And over the past decade, it has helped me build my professional network and do volunteer work that I believe has had a meaningful impact.

So, look for the right association for you, and then get involved. Every association is always looking for volunteers. If you are early in your career, you will start with some relatively menial tasks. But view it as an investment—do the tasks with good cheer, and over a couple of years you will begin to be considered a leader, a go-to individual on whom the association can rely. Not only does this help build your network, it also burnishes your reputation. Given the investment you should make in a volunteer-based organization, pick one, and only one, association to be actively involved with at any given time. You have obligations to your employer to meet first, so be careful not to over-commit yourself, which can negatively affect your performance and associated reputation across multiple organizations.

3. **Effectively Use Social Media** – Those now in the early stages of their careers have a robust set of tools that was not available when I entered the workforce. I grew up in the pre-Internet era, so I have some trepidation about commenting on the use of social media platforms and behaviors. Yet social media is an essential tool for those in the technology field. I chose LinkedIn early in its existence and have made extensive use of the platform over the past fifteen years. My use of LinkedIn does four things for me: 1) keeps me linked with members of

my network; 2) keeps members of my network abreast of my activities; 3) works to expand my network; and 4) projects a professional image for both members and non-members of my network through relevant posts and comments. I also maintain a Twitter account. I use both LinkedIn and Twitter regularly but judiciously, posting a new blog or reference to an article no more than once a month. I will like or repost others' content a few times a week. Yet, I only repost meaningful content that will be of use to my network.

Some professionals post multiple times a day about all manner of subjects. Is that the best use of their time and is that supporting them in advancing their careers? Leverage social media but do so in ways to provide meaningful information to your network members. Focus on insightful, periodic posts that help position you as professional and a thought-leader in your chosen subject.

Be of Value to Others

Having a robust professional network can greatly benefit your career. But it is a two-way street. **You need to invest in your network, and that is more than just adding new members continually. Make yourself available as support to others in your network.** For those you admire, be proactive, letting them know you can serve as a professional reference if they are looking to change positions. If some of your network members are self-employed, recognize they are most likely always looking for new business opportunities. Be another set of eyes for them, and if you spot a potential opportunity, steer it their way. Make introductions between your network members who could possibly forge mutually beneficial relationships. Don't ask for anything in return. People will remember such gestures of support for decades. While you will not get an immediate return for your generosity, it is surprising how often such gestures are paid back with some favor or introduction. And helping others in your network begins the "give back" process that will be covered in detail in Chapter 13.

Remember Your Reputation

Having an extensive professional network can be one of the most effective ways to open new opportunities and accelerate your career. But this is only the case if you have a positive reputation, one for professionalism and integrity. While the technology field is quite large and diverse, it becomes relatively small within particular subject areas. You should make sure you are on the right side of the line when it comes to having a positive reputation. This is particularly the case when it comes to integrity—your professional network can become a liability to you if the word on the street is that you are a person that lacks integrity.

Conclusion

Building and maintaining a professional network is a career-long undertaking that requires dedication and patience. But the payoff, sometimes decades later, can be profound. So by all means make it a habit to continually develop your professional network through your employer, a professional association, and social media. Whether an introvert or extrovert, if you have a sincere interest in others and show respect, the vast majority of people will respond positively. This networking will pay long-term professional and personal dividends. It has another significant benefit in the near term as well. It supports your effort to find the right mentors for you—mentors who can help you grow in your career.

Key Takeaways from Chapter 6: Develop a Network

- Building your professional network can be one of the most beneficial things you can do to succeed in your career. But it is also an endeavor that takes significant, sustained effort.

- It always makes sense to continue to invest in building and then maintaining your professional network. There are three steps you should take:

  1. **Start with Your Organization** – Work to get to know other employees throughout your organization, emphasizing developing relationships with others working in technical or process disciplines in which you have an interest.

  2. **Find the Right Professional Association** – Associations are a meaningful way to broaden your network rapidly. You should pick an association that suits you and fits well with your career goals.

  3. **Effectively Use Social Media** – Leverage social media, but do it by providing meaningful information to members of your network. Insightful, periodic posts can help position you as a thought-leader.

- You need to invest in your network. Make yourself available as support to others in your network.

- Remember your reputation—your professional network can become a liability to you if you are a person who lacks professionalism or integrity.

Building and maintaining a professional network is a career-long undertaking that requires dedication and patience. The payoff, sometimes decades later, can be profound.

Chapter 7:

Cultivate Mentors – We All Need Them

"Show me a successful individual and I'll show you someone who had real positive influences in his or her life. I don't care what you do for a living—if you do it well I'm sure there was someone cheering you on or showing the way. A mentor."

Denzel Washington

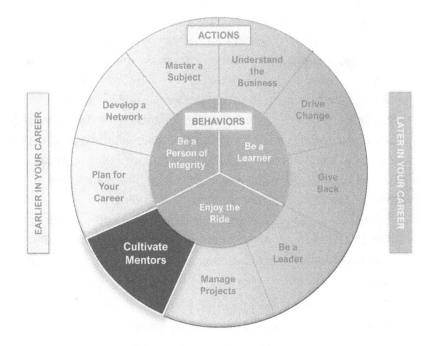

It is difficult for many of us to objectively see ourselves the way others view us. This difficulty is not limited, of course, to just those in the technology field. But when it comes to human relationships, many technologists struggle to understand others and behave in ways that will build strong, positive working relationships. Whatever your career goals, having greater self-awareness is vital to success. We all have strengths to leverage and weaknesses that need addressing. Yet many of us struggle to understand ourselves, particularly in terms of what those weaknesses are, let alone how to address them. **A mentor can be incredibly valuable in helping you understand your strengths and weaknesses.** But a mentor is not just a friend or colleague who provides you understanding. A mentor is willing to have difficult discussions with you, offering advice on how best to leverage your strengths and address your weaknesses.

I have had a number of excellent mentors during my career. And today I still count several individuals with whom I interact as mentors—people with whom I can share ideas and who offer sound advice. Early in my career, I looked for mentors who would support my growth in my technical skills, and that was very helpful. Yet I initially failed to understand the value of mentors who could help me improve my interpersonal skills. It was not until my late twenties that I finally recognized the importance of having such mentors. Interestingly, my mentors include a few individuals outside the technical field, including my wife, who have been invaluable in helping me deal with people. They are willing to have difficult discussions with me regarding my behavior and provide me specific advice on how to improve my relationships with others.

You should work to cultivate mentors in all aspects of your professional career. Be humble and recognize that you can always improve, even in areas you consider your strengths. **Make it an explicit objective to develop several mentoring re-**

lationships that can provide you coverage in all aspects of your work. This includes the subject matter you work in, the processes used in your organization to conduct the work, and the interpersonal skills needed to develop strong teams and solid working relationships.

Mentors Early in Your Career

Having mentors when you are new to your profession is essential. Early in your career, you need mentors who can provide advice and feedback in the technical or process subjects you are learning. Like an instructor or teacher in the classroom, these subject-matter mentors can help you rapidly understand many practical aspects of dealing with a particular technology or process discipline, cutting through the theory and providing you advice relevant to the work you are doing. Such mentors can also support you in career development, helping you determine the most appropriate approaches to develop expertise in a given technology or process discipline. And they may help by introducing you to other potential mentors they know that will enhance your growth and experience.

Perhaps just as crucial for you early in your career is to have a mentor who can "show you the ropes" as you learn the basics of appropriate professional behaviors in dealing with fellow employees, at all levels, of your organization. Also, such a mentor can help you deal effectively with customers and partners as well. These are essential behaviors that can propel a young person forward, particularly if you are targeting management positions and, eventually, the organization's executive ranks.

Gaining an understanding of appropriate professional behaviors is different from relationship-building. For instance, very early in your career, it is almost always the case that you are not in a management role. You are typically in support roles. As such, you need to understand and learn how to support your managers effectively and the appropriate behaviors you should exhibit in those roles. For example, if you are on a project supporting a customer, you need to be mindful of respecting and supporting the project manager. You should not take actions or make statements that undermine the project manager's views or authority. In private, one-on-one, it is acceptable to question and even disagree with the project manager, but not in front of a customer. This is a simple example, but too often, those entering the workplace have little understanding of such protocols.

Lastly, look for a mentor who will help you cultivate relationships and deal with interpersonal relationship issues. Even if you view your interpersonal skills as a strength, professional relationships differ from typical social and personal relationships. Undoubtedly, you will make good friends at work, but the large majority of your professional relationships are not about friendship. They are about having mutual respect and the capability to work well together toward achieving an objective. As such, early in your career, you ought to cultivate a mentor or two who can help you understand and deal with professional relationships.

Mentors in Mid-Career and Later in Your Career

Once you have ten years of work experience, you will have a much better understanding of your strengths and weaknesses. You will also have a more developed understanding of your career goals. You should be taking steps that enhance your capabilities and work to gain experience that supports you in meeting those career goals. Mentors should play an essential role in helping you with this discovery, giving you feedback on your goals, and working with you on the steps you should take to realize your aspirations. This is not to imply you should drop mentors you have cultivated earlier in your career—they can continue to be sounding boards for you in the areas of subject matter and relationship development.

As your career goals more fully crystallize, you will want to seek mentors who are currently, or have been, in roles you are targeting. For instance, perhaps you have been a task manager and are now taking on the leadership of small technology projects. You are enjoying this work, and it is fulfilling to deliver value to customers. You may be a person who would like to run large-scale technology programs in the future. So, you should find and cultivate a mentor who has large-scale program experience. Their perspective and advice are invaluable, because they have walked this journey before. Don't feel obliged to always take their advice or follow the path they have taken, but understanding why they made their decisions provides you useful feedback. If they are strong mentors, they will even share their mistakes and lessons learned along their journey, which is also helpful input as you plan your own journey.

The example described above involves project and program management, but even if you plan to remain an individual contributor, having mentors to support your journey is still essential. Perhaps you aspire to become a leading expert in a particular technology. Having mentors who you respect in that field will support your career development. They can help you determine what job assignments, additional training, research, and professional associations will be valuable to you.

And once you have reached a senior role and perhaps met your initial career goals, the need for having mentors does not disappear. When I took over Learning Tree International as CEO, I needed mentors who could support me as I stepped into a company that was struggling financially. So I looked for and identified an individual with extensive company turn-around experience. He had successfully turned around companies several times as a CEO. Because he had dealt with a number of situations remarkably similar to mine, he became an ideal mentor to me. In particular, he provided sound advice based on his experience with what did and did not work for him. I was also able to identify another individual with extensive experience in the technical training industry, in companies with product offerings similar to those provided by Learning Tree. This individual offered practical advice for improving our product quality and efficiency. The combination of these two mentors' guidance was quite valuable to me as the Learning Tree CEO.

Cultivating Mentors

Mentors are critically important, but they need to be the right ones. The right mentor is someone with whom you can create a trusting relationship, one in which you feel comfortable sharing your weaknesses and concerns. It is also someone who can provide you unbiased, constructive advice. The advice being unbiased is essential—you must have total confidence that your mentor gives you the best advice they can, free of any self-interest or other influence. Therefore, while you can, and should, have a mentor or two from within your organization, it is also helpful to cultivate mentors outside your organization.

The criteria to be a good mentor set a high bar, so you should expect it will take both time and effort to develop a cadre of mentors who can support you in all facets of your professional life. But how do you find suitable candidates and develop the relationships to the point where you feel confident even to ask a colleague to be a mentor? Undertake the following steps:

1. **Actively build your professional network** – Your mentors will invariably come from your professional network. The larger and more diverse your network, the more likely you will have network members who can become mentors. This is a primary benefit of building your network, particularly early in your career. But don't do this randomly. Early in your career, you should aim to have at least one men-

tor in each of the three activities described earlier: 1) subject-matter expertise; 2) appropriate business behaviors; and 3) interpersonal relationships. Think about building your network to add individuals who might support you in each of these dimensions. For instance, target a professional association that will enable you to meet people with the appropriate subject-matter expertise. You will most likely find a mentor for appropriate business behavior from someone senior in your organization. And in terms of relationships, think beyond the confines of your professional life. Sometimes, as in my case, a spouse or personal friend can be a mentor on interpersonal relationships.

2. **Assess and develop a list of possible mentors** – Most members of your professional network will not prove good fits as mentors. Again, it comes down to comfort and trust. While you should have good relations with all members of your professional network, identify those individuals with whom you have a special rapport and are very comfortable. If they also have the right experience and you respect them, both their judgment and what they have accomplished, they are excellent candidates to become mentors. Searching for mentors is not, of course, a one-time exercise. As you continue to develop your professional network, constantly assess new members of your network. And even if you decide that someone does not have the experience and insight you are looking for, years later you might find you would value that person as a mentor. It is another reason to cultivate your professional network.

3. **Ease into a more formal mentor relationship** – Even if all the signs are positive, and you know a colleague would be a good mentor, be judicious. Some individuals don't feel comfortable in a formal mentor relationship or in becoming too intimate in sharing themselves and their experiences. So,

start by asking for some advice on a small matter and make it informal, as part of a conversation. An experienced person will typically understand where this might lead, and you will quickly know if the individual is willing to become a mentor. This way, you enable an individual to back off gracefully, so you don't harm the professional relationship. If you are pleased with that initial interaction and get back thoughtful and useful advice, ask for additional guidance on another matter. There is no rule regarding when such an individual is now your mentor, but at some point, you should ask the individual if you can turn to them on a reasonably regular basis for feedback and advice.

As described earlier, you should seek to have several mentors who support different aspects of your development. While there is no exact number, be careful not to have too many mentors at any given time. You should cultivate a relationship with each one, so they get to know you well, and you can turn to them regularly to provide updates and get their feedback. Each mentor is an investment of your time. You ask for something special of them, and you need to treat them with respect and invest in the relationship. A close and strong relationship of mutual respect and honesty is a great gift, so choose and nurture each mentor with care and appreciation. It can be challenging to do that if you have lined up too many mentors.

Conclusion

Having several mentors at any given time in your career can be extremely valuable and enlightening. It is natural for us, as humans, to overplay our strengths and downplay our weaknesses. Having trusted mentors who can provide you objective feedback and advice is essential. But having mentors who can support your journey, based on their similar experiences, is even more valuable. Recognize that as you progress, the makeup of your mentors will shift. That is okay and to be expected. Remember that no matter what your seniority, mentors can still be valuable to you. Please make it a habit to continually be on the lookout for individuals who might be mentors, whether now or potentially sometime in the future.

Key Takeaways from Chapter 7: Cultivate Mentors

- It is difficult for many of us to objectively see ourselves the way others view us. We all have strengths to leverage and weaknesses that need addressing. Yet many of us struggle to understand ourselves, particularly in terms of what those weaknesses are, let alone how to address them.

- A mentor can be very valuable in helping you understand your strengths and weaknesses. But a mentor is not just a friend or colleague who provides you understanding. A mentor is willing to have difficult discussions with you, offering advice on how best to leverage your strengths and address your weaknesses.

- Early in your career, you should aim to have at least one mentor in each of these areas: 1) subject-matter expertise; 2) appropriate business behaviors; and 3) interpersonal relationships.

- How do you find suitable candidates and develop the relationships to the point where you feel confident even to ask a colleague to be a mentor? Take the following steps:

  1. **Actively build your professional network** – The larger and more diverse your network, the more likely you will have network members who could become mentors.

  2. **Assess and develop a list of possible mentors** – Identify individuals with whom you have a special rapport and who have the right experience. You must respect them, both for their judgment and what they have accomplished.

  3. **Ease into a more formal mentor relationship** – Be judicious. Some individuals don't feel comfortable in a formal mentor relationship or want to become that intimate in sharing themselves and their experiences.

Having trusted mentors who can provide you objective feedback and advice is essential. But having mentors who can support your journey, based on their similar experiences, is even more valuable.

Chapter 8:

Master a Subject – Be Considered an Expert

"Very narrow areas of expertise can be very productive. Develop your own profile. Develop your own niche."

Leigh Steinberg

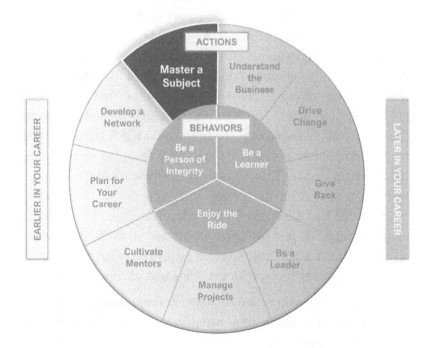

Since I entered the technology field more than thirty-five years ago, there has been an explosion in new technologies, methodologies, and processes. The Internet, object-oriented design, Agile methods leading to DevOps and DevSecOps, machine learning, and even cybersecurity did not exist in 1984. And new technologies and application options constantly emerge. The list includes: personal devices with sensor-driven assists; "smart" environmental controls, appliances and security systems; advanced software-defined networks (SDNs); robotics; new media creation and distribution tools; and artificial intelligence, to name just a few. It is a fantastic array that has led to an unprecedented number of new subject areas in technology and various positions or work roles that align with each subject. And each one offers opportunities because it requires qualified innovators, managers, and practitioners.

Take cybersecurity as one example. The National Institute of Standards and Technology (NIST), part of the U.S. Department of Commerce, is a leader in developing cybersecurity standards, including the NIST cybersecurity framework (CSF). This framework has rapidly become a "de facto" standard for cybersecurity risk management across all industries, well beyond just federal government agencies. The National Initiative for Cybersecurity Education (NICE) is an organization within NIST, and it has created a companion workforce framework for cybersecurity (the NICE Framework). This workforce framework defines seven workforce categories, thirty-three distinct areas of work, and fifty-two individual work roles. For each work role, the framework includes the KSAs and the tasks associated with that role. Organizations can use this framework to create positions by assigning roles to a position, along with the KSAs that align with each role.

So, given that there are fifty-two defined roles for cybersecurity alone, you can imagine what it looks like if you map all the IT and related disciplines—there are hundreds of different roles. And when you expand the exercise to incorporate specific product expertise (for example, establishing and administrating an application on a cloud service provider such as Amazon Web Services), the number of distinct roles is undoubtedly in the thousands. On the one hand, that appears daunting, as there is so much choice. Instead, look at it as a vast opportunity. Given this diversity, challenge yourself to become an expert in one or more of these defined roles (subject areas), and further, challenge yourself to do it relatively early in your career.

Types of Experts

Anytime during your career, but particularly early in your career, you should strive to become an expert. What does this mean? Within the technology field, there are three typical ways to become an expert:

1. **Develop the KSAs associated with a specific technology** – Most of us with engineering, computer science, mathematics, or other science backgrounds are detail-oriented. This orientation serves us well in working with technologies and related technology-based products. So being an expert here involves developing a deep understanding of the underlying technology, and if product-related, the implementation and use of that product for a customer. Some of you may even have the innate talent to advance a subject area through original research or innovation.

2. **Develop the KSAs associated with a specific process discipline** – The use of modern process disciplines is critical to success for organizations that use technology. These disciplines include project and program management (and their sub-disciplines), Agile and DevOps for the development of systems, or ITIL to support the fielding of IT systems and their support in operations. Additionally, in cybersecurity, there are process disciplines related to areas such as risk

management, cyber operations, and cyber forensics. Like technologies and products, one can become knowledgeable and proficient in using a particular process discipline.

3. **Apply technology-based solutions to address specific business challenges** – For many in our field, assuming a role that uses a technology-based product, service, or process to support a customer is a form of expertise. And this does not apply to just technologists. Some top salespeople are experts at identifying how a specific technology-based product or service can best support a customer. Sometimes, it is the analyst on a project that is the key, the one able to serve as the liaison between a customer and a technical project team. Therefore, expertise is not just about the advancement of technology or a process, but also about the correct application of technology to address business challenges.

After earning my undergraduate degree in electrical engineering, I joined SRA International. I was impressed with the knowledge and achievements of those with whom I interviewed and felt drawn to the company. I started in a small organization at SRA that was developing wide-area network optimization algorithms. At that time, it was a crucial discipline, given the relatively modest bandwidth capabilities of the telecommunications systems, along with their high cost. Therefore, it was essential to use mathematical algorithms and simulation techniques to model these systems to maximize the throughput of a wide-area network while minimizing cost. I had to learn wide-area networking, understand the state-of-the-art mathematical algorithms used for network optimization, and learn new languages and tools to develop software programs for supporting projects to optimize our customers' networks. It was demanding and intellectually stimulating work.

Given that so much of what I was learning was new, I was overwhelmed for quite a while. But sometime during my third year on the job, I was feeling more comfortable in my role. By my fifth year, I felt capable in the position, working with our customers, collecting the appropriate data, applying the right software tools, and delivering value for our customers. In retrospect, at about that five-year mark, I could have called myself an expert in doing wide-area network design. That does not mean I developed new algorithms to advance the state of wide-area network design. Instead, I applied the best capabilities available at that time to the challenge of optimizing wide-area networks. Therefore, I view my expertise in network design as the third type described above, supporting the use of technology to address a specific business challenge.

Today, given the advancements in networking technology that enable telecommunications systems to handle magnitudes more data transmission at a much-reduced cost, there is no need for the types of network designs I specialized in during the 1980s. Yet, I don't regret the years I spent early in my career specializing in network design. It taught me much about applying technology to customers' challenges, serving our customers, and managing tasks and then small projects. It turned out to be an excellent start to working in an IT professional services organization. It started me on a path that enabled me to lead larger IT projects and, eventually, large IT programs.

Striving to Become an Expert

So challenge yourself to become an expert in a subject in the technology field. It can be in a technology or process discipline or the application of solutions to address business challenges. But how do you go about identifying the subject right for you? And once you have identified a subject, what are the steps you should take?

First, as part of your career planning described in Chapter 5, identify potential subjects in which you can strive to become an expert. The subjects need to align with your long-term career goals and match well with the KSAs you are looking to develop to help you attain your long-term goals. You should also have excitement, and even passion, for the subjects you have identified. But to become an expert is not just about book learning—you need to identify subjects in which you can gain real-world experience, using the technology or process day-after-day in real-world situations. Finally, use your mentors to try out your ideas, and ask for and be open to critical feedback regarding your choices. Do your mentors believe you have innate skills to master a particular technology or discipline? Do they think it will help you to address the development of KSAs that support your long-term goals? Do they have other ideas on particular subjects that might be a better fit for you? Mentors can provide you significant help as you work through this decision.

With considerable focus and effort, you can become an expert in a chosen subject in a five-year timeframe. That fits well with my recommendation for viewing your career in five-year segments. It also works well with the development of your IDP, which should be a five-year plan.

As you work to develop an IDP that will help you become an expert in a chosen subject, first focus on the need for formal education or training. For example, returning to the cybersecurity roles, perhaps there is a subject in cybersecurity for which you have a passion. Obtaining a master's degree in cybersecurity is an option you might consider. Maybe you could also add a cybersecurity certification or two from organizations such as (ISC)^2 or ISACA. But that, in and of itself, does not qualify you as an expert. You need to develop practical skills, which require several years of hands-on experience. You should identify and join the professional association that best aligns with your efforts to develop your expertise in your chosen subject. It's there that experts in your subject assemble, and with the right involvement, you can relatively quickly get to know a number of them. Look to build your network of existing experts in your subject through a professional association. Ideally, one of those experts can serve as a mentor to you to help accelerate your development. For instance, such a mentor can point you to the publications (to include books and periodicals) in your subject that are considered most valuable.

How do you know that you have met your objective—that you are an expert in a given subject? Here are four questions to ask yourself:

1. **Are you frequently asked for the use of your expertise in a subject?** Being asked is an external validation of your knowledge and practical use of your expertise by co-workers and others in the industry. You may believe you are an expert, but there is no substitute for others explicitly acknowledging it by turning to you for that expertise.

2. **Do you personally know some of the individuals considered to be world-class in your subject?** Experts in a subject get to know and communicate with each other. They trade ideas and work together to advance the state of a particular subject. Are you part of this group in your subject area? Do you know who these world-class experts are? Do they know and respect you? Are you adding value as you interact with these other experts?

3. **Have you published an article or made public presentations related to your subject?** Beyond customer-oriented project work, are you published or have you made presentations at conferences related to your subject? These are validations of how others view you in your field.

4. **Have you contributed content to enhance the state-of-the-art in your subject?** Such contributions can vary significantly, but examples can include publishing code on "open source" projects, supporting the development of stan-

dards, or serving on a committee to document "best practices" in your subject.

Given the subjective nature of the question "Are you an expert," it is not a given that you have to answer yes to all four questions posed above to think of yourself as an expert. But you can use these questions as yardsticks regarding whether you are recognized as an expert inside as well as outside your organization.

You may be thinking, especially if you are new in your career, that achieving expert status in five years is unrealistic. You think you are too new, with too much to learn. I understand and can empathize because that is how I felt when first entering work after earning my undergraduate degree. But with technology evolving so rapidly, five years is a relatively long time in our business. With the right focused effort, you can develop your KSAs and address your behaviors to meet such an objective in five years. It will require dedication well beyond a typical 9-to-5 job, but it is possible.

The Career Benefits

Why is it so important to earn the title of expert, particularly in early to mid-career? It provides you a platform to build upon in three beneficial ways.

- Developing expertise recognized outside of your organization increases your value in the employer's eyes. In the near term, your value rises, which is then typically reflected in the opportunities you have within your organization (and in your compensation).

- Your expertise supports developing your professional network. As your reputation is enhanced, it becomes easier to build your network, getting introductions to others, both those who work directly in the subject you currently focus on and related subject areas. This can dramatically help you increase the size and value of your professional network.

- Finally, developing such expertise provides you with perspective. Once you make an effort to become an expert in a given subject, you understand the effort and the dedication it takes. If you plan, given your career goals, to move into management and hope to become an executive someday, having this perspective is quite valuable. Once in management, you will not be an expert in many of the subject areas you will oversee. Still, you will be able to better identify experts in other subjects and support those who are developing expertise. Your expertise and experience not only give you credibility, they also give you a perspective to assess and support those that work for you.

As described at the beginning of this chapter, technologies and process disciplines are continually evolving. If you begin to manage others and lead organizations, it is possible (even likely) that you will not stay current in your chosen subject. That is okay and expected. But it in no way diminishes the value of having developed expertise in a subject earlier in your career. The three benefits outlined above will endure and positively impact your career—long after the expertise you acquired early in your career is no longer of value.

Conclusion

No matter your position or background, as a professional in the technology field you support the development or delivery of solutions to address customers' challenges. And the creation, development, and fielding of such solutions require expertise in technology, products, processes, sales, and marketing—all leading to the ability to craft such solutions for a particular customer. Your value increases substantially to the degree that you can become an expert in a facet of this value chain. It is worth investing in yourself to become an expert—over a career, you will reap a substantial return on your investment.

Key Takeaways from Chapter 8: Master a Subject

- There is an unprecedented number of new subject areas in technology and various positions or work roles that align with each subject.

- Within cybersecurity alone, the NIST workforce framework for cybersecurity (the NICE Framework) defines seven workforce categories, thirty-three distinct areas of work, and fifty-two individual work roles.

- If you expand to specific product expertise, the number of distinct roles, or subjects, in the technology field is undoubtedly in the thousands.

- Anytime during your career, but particularly early in your career, you should strive to become an expert in a particular subject. Within the technology field, there are three typical ways to become an expert:

  1. **Develop the KSAs associated with a specific technology**
  2. **Develop the KSAs associated with a specific process discipline**
  3. **Apply technology-based solutions to address specific business challenges.**

- Choose a subject in which you can strive to become an expert. The subject needs to align with your long-term career goals. You should have a passion for the subject, and you must be able to gain real-world experience in your subject. Use your mentors to support you in choosing the subject and developing your plan.

- Capture as part of your IDP a five-year plan to become an expert in your chosen subject.

- Becoming an expert enhances your reputation both inside and outside your organization. In the future, the process and work required to become an expert give you a perspective to assess and support those that work for you.

It is worth investing in yourself to become an expert—over a career, you will reap a substantial return on your investment.

Chapter 9:

Manage Projects –
Understand How to
Implement Technology

"Operations keeps the lights on, strategy provides a light at the end of the tunnel, but project management is the train engine that moves the organization forward."

Joy Gumz

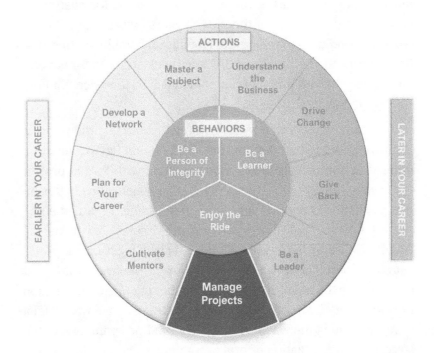

Driving change in any organization's capabilities occurs by successfully delivering projects. The Project Management Institute (PMI) defines a project as "a temporary endeavor undertaken to create a unique product, service, or result." So, whenever an organization creates a process or implements a new system, it engages in activities that define it as a project. There are other things an organization does that are also projects. For example, projects can consist of refining an existing process or even creating a written report. How an organization manages the activities that constitute a project can vary greatly by organization and type of endeavor. But for any project that involves the implementation of technology, the use of sound project management disciplines is vital for success.

As I described in Chapter 8, after college graduation I joined SRA International to work on wide-area network designs for customers. Both the development of software programs to support our design work and the designs we completed for customers constituted projects. Over the sixteen years I worked at SRA, my work broadened to include developing and implementing systems. I grew to lead significantly larger projects, both for government agencies and commercial companies in the telecommunications and finance industries.

I was on some projects and even led some that did not perform well. As I reflect on that time, SRA should have done more upfront project management training, along with formal project management mentorship, which would have helped us better organize, minimize rework, and stay on schedule. I learned some painful lessons. But those performance issues also made me acutely aware of the need for sound management of our work. During my years at SRA, I worked on dozens of projects, and that provided me the breadth of experience that put me in the position to lead major IT projects. Ultimately, that experience was crucial to my becoming the leader of the IRS's BSM program, one of the largest IT modernization efforts ever undertaken.

The Value to You

Given the importance of projects to all organizations, anyone working in the technology field should understand and learn how to manage projects. This applies to everyone in the technology field, including the researcher in the lab, software developer, or product salesperson. This recommendation may strike you as odd. You might ask why salespeople need to understand how to manage projects. The reason is that most technology-based services or products require projects to implement them in a customer environment. And a salesperson should understand and appreciate the effort it takes to ensure that a customer is satisfied with the product or service.

As I described in Chapter 5, I served as the Learning Tree International CEO for four-and-one-half years. During that time, I learned a lot about what it takes to successfully deliver a training course. It is more complicated than it appears. For example, Learning Tree has procedures for customizing training material for a course. And there are logistics for handling the course, with special procedures for courses taught at a customer's facility. (Some courses are now all-virtual or run in a hybrid virtual and in-class model.) There are procedures to sign up the attendees for a course, get them the material they need before the course begins, and handle technical issues if the course runs virtually. There are also customizable procedures for dealing with getting feedback after the course, ensuring that attendees complete online feedback surveys.

Each course Learning Tree delivers is a project. As such, there are necessary disciplines and management processes to ensure the success of each course delivery. While it is a highly repeatable project, there is a surprising number of project variations needed to support customers' requirements. Predictably, the most successful salespeople at Learning Tree understand these procedures exceptionally well and better serve their clients based on that understanding. So, while the need is not explicit, these successful salespeople have made sure they understand the steps required to manage these course-delivery projects.

So much of the value organizations (not just corporations, but also government agencies and non-profits) deliver to their customers is based on successfully delivering projects. Therefore, a project manager can provide outsized value for the organization. And in such a role, a project manager gains significant insights into how customers react to an organization's products and services and how they react to the processes to deliver those products and services. As such, a project manager has insights on how an organization can improve, particularly how to optimize the processes used for delivering its products and services.

Becoming a Project Manager

Early in your career, within the first ten years, you should invest in learning project management skills, putting yourself in a position to manage small projects. To do so, undertake the following steps:

1. **Earn project management credentials** – There are several different project management credentials that you can earn. In the United States, the Project Management Institute (PMI) is the predominant organization setting project management standards and offering related training courses and certifications. This institute has existed for decades and continues to evolve. It provides the Project Management Body of Knowledge (PMBOK), which is currently in its sixth edition. The PMBOK is generic, including the project management processes and knowledge areas needed for all projects, from construction to business process optimization to IT systems development. The current PMBOK outlines five project management processes: project initiation, planning, execution, monitoring and controlling, and closing. Along with these

processes, the PMBOK defines ten knowledge areas, including scope, time, cost, risk, and procurement management.

PMI's training and certification programs include the Certified Associate in Project Management (CAPM) and the Project Management Professional (PMP). If you are very early in your career, you should first earn the CAPM, as it is a stepping-stone to the more rigorous PMP, and it does not require project management work experience. In addition to formal project management training and the passing of an exam, the PMP requires work experience, which varies by the amount of your formal education. For instance, if you hold at least a bachelor's degree, you need to have thirty-six months of unique, non-overlapping project management experience, as well as 4,500 hours spent leading and directing projects.

In some other parts of the world, particularly in Europe, PRINCE2 (standing for **PR**ojects **IN** **C**ontrolled **E**nvironments) is a more popular standard for project management. Similar to PMI, it has a project management methodology and a set of professional certifications. Like the CAPM, the PRINCE2 Foundation certification is for those with basic project management skills and experience. The PRINCE2 Practitioner credential is for project management professionals, similar to the PMP.

Other organizations offer project management credentials, and universities also now offer programs. So do your homework, taking into consideration your geographic location, your industry, and which program and certification (or even college degree) best fit your career plans. Capture your desired approach in your IDP and share your plans with your employer and your mentors.

2. **Proactively work to get task and project management experience** – Formal project management education or

training is critical. It is the foundation by which you learn how to manage. Yet, it can never replace real-world experience. Organizations will often over-rely on credentials, putting individuals in positions where they fail for lack of having the necessary experience. Early in your career, you will most likely be part of a project team. It might not be called that, nor may the team leader use standard project management terminology and methods, but if you are part of a team producing a deliverable, it is a project. Take advantage of these opportunities by studying how your team leader manages, focusing on what works, and identifying areas for improvement.

To become a project manager, you must go beyond just serving on project teams. Early in your career, work to find an opportunity to lead, not at a project level, but taking on some task within a project. If possible, lead a task for which you have the underlying capability to execute. Given that you have no management experience at this point in your career, your credibility to manage a task is related to how well you can execute crucial elements of that task. For example, perhaps you have been out of college for a couple of years, and you have been a test specialist on several system implementations for your employer. At this point, you may be ready to step into a role managing a task, perhaps taking responsibility for a small team testing a subsystem. This next logical step will begin to stretch your expertise in new ways, yet keeping you anchored in processes and tools you understand well. It gives you a good chance for success in your first management assignment.

Once you have had several task management successes, you are in a position to ask for your first project management assignment. There is a difference between task and project management. As a task manager, your key stakeholder is the project manager. Once you are a project manager, your key stakeholder becomes the customer (which may be external or internal to your organization). Having a customer is a significant difference and it requires a project manager to use the full range of project management disciplines. So, before stepping up to your first project management position, you should complete formal training with a certification, such as earning the CAPM or PRINCE2 Foundation. A certification will give you a basic understanding of the range of those disciplines required to successfully manage a project.

3. **Find a project management mentor** – Very early in your career, look to build a mentor relationship with a project manager in your organization. The use of a mentor is another means for you to bolster your preparedness as you look to step into task and then project management. Those that do not manage others typically have a naïve view of what is required to be successful. They underestimate the skills and amount of work necessary to effectively motivate others, resolve conflicts, and develop an environment in which teamwork can thrive. Remain humble and keep your confidence in-check. Find a project manager whose style and capabilities you admire, and see if you can build a mentor-mentee relationship. As you begin to manage tasks, you then have someone who can provide you with sound advice on managing and leading others. Having such a mentor at this stage in your career will yield you meaningful benefits.

Stepping Beyond Basic Project Management

To reiterate, if you are in the technology field, you should learn the basic project management disciplines, and early in your career, you should apply those disciplines at a task and small-project level. If you aspire to individual contributor-oriented positions, this provides you the needed understanding to effectively work on projects.

If you aspire to positions that will require responsibilities to lead ever-larger organizations, you should continue to enhance your skills and experience in project management through specialization. Agile techniques have become the preferred approach when developing system applications, particularly those with human-machine interaction. There are techniques, including Scrum, Kanban, DevOps, and DevSecOps, to manage these types of projects. And there are organizations that focus on training and certifications for these disciplines. Additionally, several techniques, such as Scaled Agile Framework (SAFe), are used to scale Agile across an enterprise. Such disciplines will continue to evolve over the next decade, and new disciplines will emerge that will further enhance technology-based project management. What disciplines you should focus on will depend on what your organization chooses and what is considered best practice in your particular subject area.

There is a larger point regarding project management. Undoubtedly, having generic project management skills and experience is of significant value to you, but it is not sufficient to guarantee project success. Just as you should take on your first task management responsibility in an area where you have subject knowledge, it is critical to have a grasp of the issues encompassing any project you will manage. Ideally, as a project manager, you will have had significant experience working on projects in the same subject area. If you do not have that subject-area expertise, it is even more important that other key members of your project team have the requisite subject area background. One of the most critical disciplines in project management is risk management. Forming an experienced project management team, one in which the members have delivered similar projects, is the best risk-mitigation approach.

Program Management

According to PMI, a program is "a group of related projects managed in a coordinated manner to obtain benefits not available from managing them individually." Therefore, the disciplines used to manage a program are related to, although somewhat different from, project management. When managing programs, in addition to ensuring that each attendant project reaches its objective, you have to manage the interdependencies and integration between these projects. You must also ensure the program and all attendant projects are collectively meeting enterprise and portfolio objectives. To become an experienced program manager, you first need to have significant experience and expertise in managing projects.

If you aspire to senior executive roles in your career, consider investing in becoming a program manager. Almost any significant change initiative requires an organization to undertake and successfully deliver a major program. As a program manager, you can build a reputation for being a change agent. Yet large programs are the most complex and riskiest endeavors any organization undertakes. Again, risk management is key to success, both for you and the organization. If your organization offers you a critical program management role, make sure you are prepared, both in expertise and relevant experience. Success at this level in an organization can catapult a career. Unfortunately, a failure can also have a lasting impact. Chapter 12 covers the important, related topic of driving change in an organization.

Conclusion

Given the importance of projects in the technology field, everyone in the field should understand and gain experience in the basics of project management. This experience can support you no matter your position, from manager to individual contributor and from die-hard technologist to salesperson. Making this investment in learning the discipline of project management, especially early in your career, will pay you dividends in ways you cannot imagine. Project management experience provided wonderful opportunities for me, and those opportunities eventually helped me attain my career goals. It can just as well help you achieve your career goals.

Key Takeaways from Chapter 9: Manage Projects

- Driving change in any organization's capabilities occurs by successfully delivering projects. And for any project that involves the implementation of technology, the use of sound project management disciplines is vital for success.

- Given the importance of projects to all organizations, anyone working in the technology field, including researchers, software developers, and product salespeople, should understand and even learn how to manage projects.

- Early in your career, invest in learning project management skills. To do so, undertake the following steps:

  1. **Earn a project management credential** – Formal training via PMI, PRINCE2, or a university program will provide you with the required foundational knowledge.

  2. **Proactively work to get task and project management experience** – Seek out task management opportunities to develop your management capabilities prior to stepping into a project management position.

  3. **Find a project management mentor** – Find a project manager whose style and capabilities you admire and see if you can build a mentor-mentee relationship.

- If you aspire to positions that will require responsibilities to lead ever-larger organizations, you should continue to enhance your skills and experience in project management through specialization. Agile techniques have become the preferred approach when developing system applications, particularly those with human-machine interaction.

- If you aspire to senior executive roles in your career, consider investing in becoming a program manager. Almost all significant change initiatives require an organization to undertake and successfully deliver a major program.

Investing in learning the discipline of project management, especially earlier in your career, will pay you dividends in ways you cannot imagine.

Later in Your Career

Chapter 10

Understand the Business – Apply Technology to Create Value

"The technology you use impresses no one. The experience you create with it is everything."

Sean Gerety

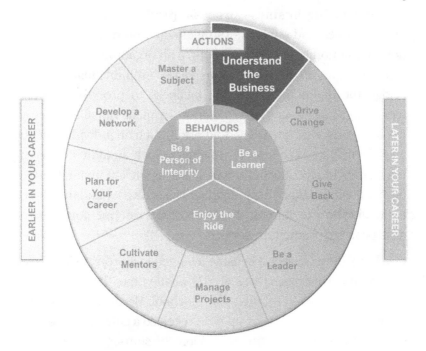

For almost all of us in the technology field, our work supports furthering the interest of a customer or constituent. They may be external or internal to your organization, but rarely does work in technology and technology-based solutions exist without customers or constituents. Whether it is working to advance the state of a particular technology, develop products to address a specific business process, or offer services to implement a solution, our work supports addressing or enhancing a business process, product, or service. As an example, virtually every company, government agency, and non-profit organization uses software products to support its finance operations, a core business function. Modern finance and accounting would not be possible without these tools. In this example, the finance team, typically led by a chief financial officer (CFO), is the internal customer.

The value is not in the technology-based solutions themselves. The value is in how those solutions improve the underlying business process, product, or service. The proper choice and successful implementation of the right technology solution to enhance aspects of an organization's business processes can create tremendous value. An individual who can bridge the technology with the business to propose effective technology-based solutions is one of the most valuable employees in an organization today. And often, such an individual is not an executive or even a senior manager. Such an individual is often an individual contributor who has a significant understanding of that business. And this individual has creativity and the ability to imagine how technology-based solutions can transform a business process, product, or service.

Early in my career, I became involved in a project supporting a start-up corporation. I was at SRA at the time, the professional services corporation I joined out of school. Because of an investment SRA made in the start-up, SRA received a contract to develop a technology-based solution to support the start-up's service delivery capabilities. Before investing, SRA assigned one of its senior system engineers to support the due diligence efforts and development of the solution's technical architecture. Once the project started, he served as the lead system engineer and architect.

This senior system engineer taught me a lot about creating value. He had a deep technical understanding and skills across multiple technical disciplines. But to develop a solution for this start-up, he intently studied the start-up's business plan and the industry it was designed to serve. He was able to architect and support developing a solution that was scalable to meet their needs and enabled the fledgling company to go to market. Four years later, the start-up sold for a manifold return on investment for SRA and other investors. While indeed a team effort, I credit this senior system engineer as the one most responsible for the value we created. I valued his capabilities so highly that when I served as the IRS CIO, I hired him as a consultant to support our system engineering team as its members developed modernization plans for several of the core legacy systems.

Understand How Your Organization Creates Value

All organizations exist to create and provide value to customers or constituents. The value may be embodied in a stand-alone product produced and sold by the organization, or the value may be a service, either stand-alone or part of a complex value chain consisting of services and products from multiple organizations. Similarly, there is an extensive range of types and number of customers or constituents that benefit from the value an organization creates. At an extreme, some organizations focus exclusively on primary research, looking to advance the state of science or a discipline for all of society. At the other end of the spectrum, some organizations, based on their unique expertise, focus on serving a single customer, such as a large corporation or government agency.

Within an organization of any scale, there are sub-organizations (departments) that provide specific value. Sometimes that value can be for external customers, but often departments exist as part of an organization's value chain. The value they create and the customer they serve is often another department within the larger organization. I am often surprised at how many employees struggle to articulate the actual value their parent organization creates and how the value is received and leveraged by a customer. Employees become focused very narrowly on their specific jobs, and sometimes they even struggle to articulate how their departments benefit the larger organization.

Early in your career, your focus is understandably more oriented on your professional development. Your focus should be on developing your career plan and IDP, building your professional network, and developing expertise in a subject. As you reach mid-career, and certainly later in your career, your focus and the value you provide often shift. Your ability to support your organization's reason for being, to support its creation of value, becomes paramount. And this applies whether you are a senior executive, such as a CIO, or an individual contributor, such as a senior system engineer or senior business analyst. The more senior you are in an organization, the more your success becomes ever-more aligned with your role in supporting its value-creation abilities.

As you advance, either in management or as an individual contributor, you should study your organization. If you are a member of a sub-organization (a department) within a larger organization, start with the department. However, you will need to ultimately understand the value creation process at multiple levels—certainly within your department and at least one organization above your department. How do you go about this? Undertake the following two steps:

1. **Articulate your organization's value** – Start with the basics. What is the value that your organization provides? Who

is the customer? How does the customer use the product or service that creates the value? And how does the customer measure the quality of the value provided? Keep in mind that the customer might be external to the organization, but it may be an internal customer. You must be quite specific in this exercise, and you need to document it in writing.

Within a sub-organization (at a department level), this is typically a straightforward exercise as each department usually has a specific function they provide to the organization. In smaller and mid-sized organizations, there will typically be just two levels, with several departments forming the parent organization. However, in larger organizations, there are generally additional levels. For example, a set of departments may create a business line that offers a particular product or service—the combination of the business lines constitutes the entire organization. Except for senior executives who have organization-wide responsibilities, conduct this exercise within your department, as well as within one level above your department.

2. **Describe how that value is created and delivered** – This work is critical. You should document how that value is created, first in your department and in the level above. What are the specific business processes executed to create the value? Document the steps in each process and, to the degree you can, determine both who is involved in implementing each step and what systems or other technologies support its execution. Also, note when a step directly affects the customer in some manner. And when there is a step that affects the customer, document how it supports delivering value for the customer. Also, document what is considered acceptable performance and what is regarded as exceptional performance in creating value for the customer.

In essence, you are developing a deep understanding of how your organization creates and delivers its value. This exercise will typically force you to learn about disciplines far removed from your subject expertise. When I agreed to join the IRS, I knew nothing about tax administration. Using the approach outlined above, I took it upon myself to learn the IRS's business functions, their value, and the processes and related IT systems that support all facets of tax administration. I studied reports and other documentation on the IRS's tax administration processes. Further, I was inquisitive, asking numerous questions about the business and getting advice from IRS business leaders on how best to learn more. By the end of my second year at the IRS, I felt I had a good grasp of these processes. I would never claim to be an expert in any of these processes, but my knowledge proved valuable.

Interestingly, about two-and-a-half years after joining the IRS, my boss, the IRS CIO, decided to leave the agency for personal reasons. The IRS Commissioner offered me the CIO job, and I accepted. I remember speaking to the Commissioner soon after I became the CIO. He stated that a key reason he offered me the job was that I had come to understand the business processes of the IRS as well as many of the operations executives. On reflection, I view that statement as one of the best compliments I have received in my professional career. It was an acknowledgment of the work I put into understanding the IRS business. As a senior IT executive, I viewed my job as working to ensure that our IT solutions and services best supported the IRS's business needs. Having a solid understanding of the IRS business processes helped me do my job effectively when running the BSM program, but even more so as the IRS CIO.

Applying Your Understanding

If you have invested in understanding the organization at the level described above, you will have significant insights into its challenges. Furthermore, you will have insights into how the organization can improve by leveraging technology. You may even have proposed approaches regarding how the organization can undergo a digital transformation, reimagining a business process that can radically and positively impact the organization.

As technologists, however, we need to be especially careful in presenting ideas that will significantly impact a business process or outcome. Organizations often fail to implement good ideas. In order for an idea to be implemented, it must be introduced and positioned correctly, and the right stakeholders need to be involved. As technologists, we must be particularly careful in introducing an idea because, typically, the business is not our domain, no matter how much we might work to understand it. On the other hand, do not sit on good ideas, never giving them a chance to be considered.

Trust and collaboration become key to introducing an idea. **As a technologist, you should seek to build trust with partners on the business side of the organization.** At the IRS, I spent a lot of time working to ensure the IRS business leaders understood that all I was doing was for the IRS's benefit—I had no other motivation. A significant part of building that trust was collaboration. I worked to develop strong partnerships with executives across all the IRS business units. These were individuals with whom I could share ideas privately and get feedback. Getting such feedback decreased the chance I would make a mistake and enhanced my understanding of the IRS business operations. Some of my ideas had been tried before, without success. Through my partnership with the business executives, I was able to answer questions like: If an idea did not work, why? What were the constraints or obstacles that caused the idea to fail?

Building relationships and working closely with business executives had another significant benefit. I would work to refine improvement ideas with these business executives. Ultimately, to be considered, an idea for a business process improvement needed to be introduced and sponsored by an executive within the business. Even as CIO, I lacked credibility with the business executives, most of whom had spent their careers at the IRS. Other IRS technologists and I could serve as the backup to a business executive, confirming that we could implement the technical changes required to implement the idea.

Your situation may be different than mine was at the IRS. Perhaps you have been at your organization for a long time and have the respect of the business executives. Or maybe you are a business executive in the organization, with your company providing technology-based products or services. Whatever your situation, building trust through collaboration is key to enabling your idea for improving a business process, product, or service to become a reality. Chapter 12 will further explore the related topic of driving substantial change in an organization.

Conclusion

Rewards come to those who create value. And for us in the technology field, significant value can be created by leveraging technology and technology-based solutions to address business challenges, whether the organization is a private-sector corporation, a government agency, or a non-profit. So as your career evolves, if you can straddle the business and technology, understanding how technology-based products and solutions can address your organization's business challenges, you can create significant value for your organization and yourself. It takes dedicated study to understand the business, and finesse to ensure your ideas can become a reality. Whatever your title, this is a way to become one of the most valued and successful members of any organization.

Key Takeaways from Chapter 10: Understand the Business

- Real value is not in the technology-based solutions themselves. The value is in how those solutions improve the underlying business process, product, or service.

- An individual who can bridge the technology with the business to propose effective technology-based solutions is one of the most valuable employees in an organization. This individual needs creativity and the ability to imagine how technology-based solutions can transform a business process, product, or service.

- As you advance, either in management or as an individual contributor, you should study your organization. If you are a member of a sub-organization (a department) within a larger organization, start with the department. However, you will need to ultimately understand the value creation process at multiple levels—certainly within your department and at least one organization above your department. Take the following steps:

  1. **Articulate your organization's value** – What is the value that your organization provides? Who is the customer? How does the customer use the product or service that creates the value?

  2. **Describe how that value is created and delivered** – What specific business processes are executed to create the value? Document the steps in each process, and to the degree you can, determine both who is involved in implementing each step and what systems or other technologies support its execution.

- How to position and introduce an idea, and who to involve, are critical factors determining whether a good idea to improve a business process, product, or service ever becomes a reality.

- As a technologist, you should build trust with partners on the business side of the organization. Building trust through collaboration is key to enabling your idea for improving a business process, product, or service to become a reality.

Become an individual who can straddle the business and technology, understanding how technology-based products and solutions can address your organization's business challenges.

Chapter 11:

Be a Leader –
Work at It

"The first responsibility of a leader is to define reality. The last is to say thank you. In between the two, the leader must become a servant and a debtor. That sums up the progress of an artful leader."

Max DePree

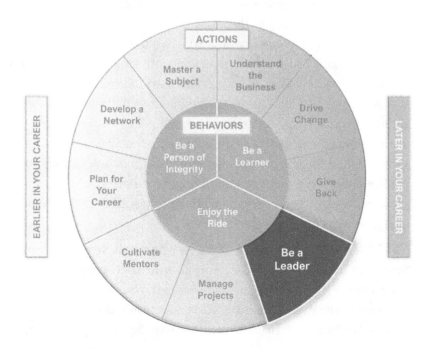

For many people, particularly in mid- or later-career, your career path plan will include leading organizations and managing people. While many people in the technology field are excellent leaders, many of us with technology backgrounds struggle to understand and incorporate some aspects of leadership. We are sometimes more at ease with topics that demand precision and factual answers, including the "hard" sciences, such as physics and chemistry. On the other hand, leading a group of people can be difficult, as you seek to understand their thinking, motivations, and actions. How do you provide leadership when chances are they don't understand you either? I am an example of someone who has struggled with leading people. Being an engineer, introverted, and with a type-A personality, I have found it difficult to relate to many people. Therefore, I have struggled to understand co-workers' positions and sometimes found it challenging to motivate them.

Early in my career, one of my mentors noted that he felt first-line management was the most challenging management position. As a new manager, you don't have a lot of management experience, and you are often managing individuals early in their careers. This lack of experience on the part of both the manager and employee can lead to misunderstandings and inappropriate actions on both sides. Based on my experiences, I agree with my mentor. Once I was in the position of being the manager of managers, I found there were significantly fewer misunderstandings. While we didn't always agree on the right course of action, I rarely had misunderstandings or an inability to resolve issues dealing with managers who reported to me.

Given the challenges you face when you step into any first-line management role, you should take steps to prepare yourself. And this is true even if you consider yourself someone who is a natural leader and has the innate capability to motivate others. There are leadership and management techniques we all can learn. Here again, I made a mistake in my career. Because I had no formal leadership or management training as I stepped into my first people leadership role, I struggled in some situations. It wasn't until years after assuming my first leadership role that I had formal management and leadership training. I overcame this mistake, but formal training would have positioned me to handle certain situations more professionally. It also would likely have resulted in better outcomes.

Becoming a Manager

Leadership and management are two different but related disciplines. According to the Management Study Guide, leadership is "the potential to influence and drive the group efforts towards the accomplishment of goals." Management focuses on "the activities of planning, organizing, staffing, directing, and controlling resources to achieve an objective." But given that some of the resources to manage typically include people, good leadership is an essential part of good management, particularly as it relates to directing people. To get effective results from people, you need to ensure that they understand their roles, and you should inspire and motivate them, thus creating a team focused on attaining an objective. These are all aspects of leadership.

Good management starts with the ability to manage yourself and your activities. How do you plan, organize, and control yourself? At the early stages in our careers, many of us have not yet learned good habits when it comes to self-management. And at times, this is difficult for us to see in ourselves. So, ask your mentors. If this is an area that needs your attention, there are many on-demand or instructor-led courses in managing yourself, including topics such as prioritization and time management. There are also books specific to this topic.

In Chapter 9, I recommended that you learn and become proficient in project management, because it provides you many benefits in the technology field. One of those benefits is that it gives you a set of tools to support planning, organizing, and controlling resources for all types of management activities. Therefore, it benefits you in areas well beyond just project management. And if you take more advanced project management courses, you'll explore a wide array of issues related to people management and leadership. If you aspire to manage organizations of almost any scale, honing your project management skills will be a tremendous benefit.

As you progress and move into a front-line, full-time management role, augment your project management training with formal coursework on people management. Often, if you work for a larger organization, your company will offer a formal training program for new managers. Some of this training will be specific to that organization's processes (such as handling performance reviews). Still, employers often will include training on motivating employees and dealing with sensitive personnel situations. Take full advantage of these courses, or seek out external courses on people management.

Before embarking on your first full-time people-management role, you should attempt to line up a mentor or two who can support you. Ideally, you would have one mentor from within your organization and someone independent of your current organization. Both mentors should have extensive people management backgrounds. They should also meet the criteria laid out in Chapter 7 regarding mentors—namely, they are people you respect, and they are willing to provide you constructive advice. Making the shift from an individual contributor to a manager is a crucial time in your career—it is essential to have the support of mentors.

Becoming a Leader

Think of management as a skillset you can obtain. You take formal training, gain valuable experience by being in management roles of increasing importance, and use your mentors to support your growth. Think of leadership as an art, in that there is no one right way to lead. There are different formal leadership models. If you wish to rise to an organization's executive levels, you will need to choose a model that fits best with your personality and value system. Many people do not study leadership models, but they find things that work for them through trial and error. For some, this can be highly effective, but for most, it is a process that leads to many mistakes along the way and often does not maximize the individual's leadership capabilities.

As you begin to move up the management ranks, study leadership models, understand their pros and cons, and work to develop a personalized model that maximizes your leadership effectiveness. Below is a list of leadership models and descriptions taken from a Learning Tree course dealing with the topic.

Leadership Model	Leader Belief	Leader Value
Theory X	Most people must be coerced, controlled, or threatened	Obedience
Theory Y	People will exercise self-direction to achieve goals	Responsibility
The Great Man Theory	"It is far safer to be feared than loved"	Excellence
The Mintzberg Management/Leadership Model	The 10 Activities to perform: lead, liaison, figurehead, monitor, disseminator, spokesperson, resource allocator, entrepreneur, negotiator, disturbance handler	Teamwork
Situational Leadership	Directing, coaching, supporting, motivating, delegating, trusting	Honesty
Leader-Member Exchange Theory	The *in-group*—a small number of trusted followers who function as assistants, lieutenants, and advisors The *out-group*—for which there is little mutual influence	Loyalty
Transformational Leadership	Oriented toward strategy and long-term goals	Transcendence of Organizational Goals
Servant Leadership	Obstacles must be removed to allow teams to thrive	Humility
Agile Leadership	The litmus test of all business actions must be the addition of value to stakeholders	The Agile Manifesto

Various Leadership Models Used in the Technology Field

As you read through this list, some of these leadership models might strike you as inappropriate—they are not leadership traits you wish to exhibit. For instance, while I certainly value loyalty to a point, I would never want to lead via a small cadre, or inner circle. Not only does it not fit my personality, but I do not believe it to be an effective leadership style in technology-related work. However, for some, such a leadership model does work effectively.

In reality, most of us use a combination of several of these models. Different models can work in different situations, and at times, you may adopt a model to address a particular situation or when dealing with a certain type of individual. Your ability to recognize which model works in a given situation and effectively use that model is the mark of an excellent leader.

There are many different types of leaders with all manner of personalities and motivations. A leader typically has a dominant leadership model they are comfortable with, and then they diversify as needed. I use servant leadership as my primary leadership model. As I moved into management roles early in my career, I recognized my success rested mainly on the shoulders of those who reported to me. Therefore, I believe in supporting my direct reports, helping them to be successful in their own right by removing barriers, and providing guidance and help. That does not mean I neglect my responsibilities to set the vision and strategy for the organization. But in essence, I work to build a strong team of direct reports, all of whom, over time, can grow to become successful leaders. It also means, for the good of the organization, that if I determine a direct report does not have the innate skills or behaviors to be successful in their role, they must be removed from that role and done so expeditiously. It is best for such an individual to find a position in which they can be successful. And it is best for the organization.

What primary leadership model is right for me may not be suitable for you. Determining what primary model works for you is your assignment, and the earlier you do so, the better. Closely observe and learn from the leadership styles of your supervisors. What works well for them, and what does not work? And try to determine why. Also, take leadership courses, read books on the subject, and rely on your mentors. And if your organization is willing to invest in your management and leadership development, a management or executive coach can be of value to you. A coach typically has both extensive management and leadership experience and has training in how to work with rising executives, with tools and techniques to help rising executives identify the appropriate leadership model that will work best for them.

Whether using mentors or a coach, present to them the challenges you currently face to get their advice. And use them to do post-mortems on how you handled particular situations. This type of dissection of past decisions and their consequences can help you refine your leadership capabilities, both in your primary leadership model and how you should fine-tune your leadership approach, given certain situations and types of people.

Finally, whatever your management level, obtain feedback from your direct reports regarding their views on your management and leadership capabilities. Of course, getting unbiased feedback can be difficult, because direct reports are often reticent to criticize their immediate supervisors. So many organizations have implemented some version of 360-degree reviews, in which an individual's supervisor, peers, and direct reports can provide feedback anonymously. Such feedback, when first received, can be challenging to accept. Yet, the feedback offers self-awareness, highlighting weaknesses in management and leadership capabilities. And such feedback can support you as you work to refine your management and leadership style, and how to adapt it to particular situations.

Conclusion

If you want to transition from being an individual contributor to being a manager and leader of people, work at it before stepping into such management roles. You owe it to yourself and to those you will lead. Document your aspirations for management in your career plan. In your IDP, document what you will do to get ready—formal training, reading, and self-exploration. As part of your plan, make it a priority to gain skills and experience in project management. And rely on your mentors, and if possible, a coach. They can be incredibly valuable in aiding you in determining the steps you should take to prepare yourself when taking on a new management role.

As you have management success, continue to improve your leadership capabilities. Work to understand and apply various leadership models, improving your agility in handling all manner of workforce challenges. Such leadership agility, together with appropriate subject-matter knowledge, prepares you to hold the senior-most positions in an organization.

Key Takeaways from Chapter 11: Be a Leader

- There are undoubtedly many people in the technology field who are excellent leaders. But many of us with technology backgrounds struggle with aspects of leading people. Given the challenges you face when you step into any first-line management role, take steps to prepare yourself.

- Given that some of the resources you manage typically include people, good leadership is an essential part of good management, particularly as it relates to directing people.

- Good management starts with the ability to manage yourself and your activities. How do you plan, organize, and control yourself? If this is an area that needs attention, there are many courses in managing yourself, including courses on prioritization and time management. There are also books specific to this topic.

- As you progress and move into a front-line full-time management role, augment your project management training with formal coursework on people management. You should attempt to line up mentors who can support you. And if your organization is willing to invest in your development, a management or executive coach can be of value to you.

- Think of leadership as an art. There are different leadership models. If you wish to rise to an organization's executive level, you will need to choose a model that fits best with your personality and value system.

- Learn to adapt your leadership model to address particular situations or deal with certain types of people. Your ability to recognize what model works in a given situation and effectively use that model is the mark of an excellent leader.

Continue to improve your leadership capabilities. Work to understand and apply various leadership models, improving your ability to handle all manner of workforce challenges.

Chapter 12:

Drive Change – Start on the Inside

"Culture does not change because we desire to change it. Culture changes when the organization is transformed—the culture reflects the realities of people working together every day."

Frances Hesselbein

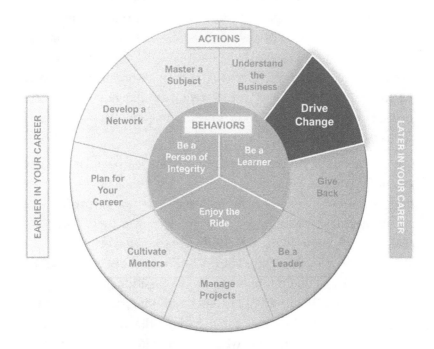

W hat is organizational culture? According to the Society for Human Resource Management (SHRM), organizational culture:

"...defines the proper way to behave within the organization. This culture consists of shared beliefs and values established by leaders and then communicated and reinforced through various methods, ultimately shaping employee perceptions, behaviors, and understanding."

Many successful organizations thrive because of their cultures. In particular, cultures that enable organizations to adapt and grow are at the root of some private-sector companies' longevity, enabling them to reinvent themselves several times over decades. But too often, organizations develop cultures resistant to change. These organizations rely on and even celebrate what worked for them in the past. In today's environment, in which digital transformation of business processes is ongoing at an unprecedented rate, a risk-averse culture can be very harmful to an organization, and in some cases, threaten an organization's very existence. Yet, to change culture requires changing the perceptions, behaviors, and understanding of the employees—you can't dictate cultural change.

For example, many government agencies have risk-averse cultures. With no competition for the services agencies provide and no fear of "going out of business," it is not surprising that many agencies develop risk-averse cultures over time. This point was brought home to me when I first entered government at the IRS to take over the leadership of the troubled BSM program. Interestingly, when I interviewed for the position, IRS leadership acknowledged the program needed revamping, and they wanted an executive from the outside to help drive the necessary change. They looked for someone who had considerable IT program management experience and had successfully driven change in private-sector corporations.

I entered the IRS with twenty years of private-sector experience, and I spent about eight of those years supporting government agencies as a contractor. While not having worked directly in government, I worked closely with several government agencies. Given my experience and the mandate to drive change, I took what I felt was a balanced approach in my first months at IRS. I knew I had a lot to learn, yet I also felt pressure to drive change fairly quickly. This turned out to be a mistake; I underestimated the influence of the IRS's culture. About four months into my tenure, my boss (the IRS CIO) took me out to lunch. He floored me when he said that if I continued to behave as I was, I would probably be out of the IRS in another couple of months. In my twenty years of professional life, I had never had a conversation like this one. I knew I was acting professionally, but I was significantly out-of-pace with the IRS culture in my zeal to drive change. And this was true even though they had hired me to drive the change I was now being criticized for making.

This was a pivotal moment in my career. Was I willing to adapt to the situation and work within the IRS's culture? I spoke with one of my mentors and did a lot of self-reflection over the next few days. I concluded that this was too important, both to the IRS and myself. It would set the IRS back if they needed to replace me so soon after I started as the BSM program lead, and it would potentially harm my career as well. I decided to adjust my approach. I knew that changing the program was required, but I needed to do it with a more collaborative approach, ensuring all key stakeholders of the BSM program were involved and consulted. Furthermore, I needed to temper my expectations regarding what could be accomplished and when.

As I reflect on my eventual four-and-one-half year tenure at the IRS, it was a learning experience for me. **It taught me about the need to work within a culture if you wish to effect change and the power of an organization once senior**

leadership aligns on the need for such change. Working as a team, we turned the BSM program around, producing significant value by successfully delivering several crucial projects in the IRS BSM portfolio. And for myself, I was promoted twice when I was at the IRS, first to become the CIO, and then the deputy commissioner for operations support, the number three position in the agency.

Driving Change

As I noted in Chapter 10 on understanding the business, as a technologist you have an outsized opportunity to support your organization by leveraging technology and technology-based solutions and services. But having a good business transformation idea is not enough. You have to collaborate across your organization and champion such an idea for it to become a reality. By partnering with the right business executives, you build trust and can bring the idea to life. This approach can work well at an individual business process or system level. And it applies to anyone driving technology-based change in an organization, from the lowest position up to the CEO. But what if you are in a leadership role and need to drive significant change in your organization? Perhaps you have taken over a struggling company in need of a turn-around, or you wish to significantly increase the performance measures of your department or business line, whether you're in a private-sector company, government agency, or non-profit organization. In these cases, you must be a change agent.

How do you go about that? Suppose the organization is in a "burning platform" situation, in which it must undergo radical change to save itself. In that case, you are free to take extreme steps that likely are not in line with the organizational culture. In such a desperate situation, the employees recognize the need for change, and employees are looking for new leadership.

However, having such a mandate for change is unusual. Typically, an organization is not in imminent danger, so there are varying views regarding what changes, if any, are required. Many organizations struggle to gain leadership consensus regarding the right changes to enhance an organization's performance. If you want to be a successful change agent, you must win over the organization's leadership to support such change. Don't be naïve regarding what this means—even if you are the organization's CEO, you need to work to ensure all of your direct reports are onboard with your proposed set of changes, or they can undermine the effort.

As a change agent, you should undertake the following steps:

1. **Understand your business** – For most organizations that are struggling, or at best treading water, there are ample opportunities to leverage technology-based solutions and services to improve an organization's performance. What you advocate depends on the organization and its current status, which brings us back to the recommendations in Chapter 10 regarding understanding the business. As a change agent, you must first invest in gaining a deep understanding of your organization's business operations. Taking this action alone will help you develop a rapport and build trust with leaders in the business.

2. **Understand and work within the organizational culture** – A change agent must convince other employees of the benefits of the changes you advocate. How best to do that? It requires building trust, and to do so, you must honor the positive aspects of the organization's culture. It also requires time. As my experience at the IRS demonstrated, you modify your behavior to fit within the organization's culture (never compromising your integrity as described in Chapter 2) to build trust and give yourself a chance to develop early successes.

3. **Study, adopt, and tailor a specific organizational change management (OCM) methodology** – OCM is a field unto itself. So you should study some of the leading OCM methodologies (this can include Kotter's 8 Steps of Change, Bridges Transition Model, and the Prosci Process). No particular OCM methodology is best. Yet, whatever the methodology, when facing a real-life situation, you will have to adapt what you have learned to the specifics of the conditions you face. That is why looking across OCM approaches is beneficial. By first making an effort to understand the business and understand the organizational culture, you will be in a good position to assess and decide which OCM methodology (or combination of methodologies) best fits your particular situation.

4. **Develop a transformation plan** – As a next step, leverage your chosen OCM methodology to develop a transformation plan, but only with the business leaders' support and collaboration. This transformation plan should be a tailored, step-by-step approach to driving the changes in business operations and related IT systems. As the OCM methodologies note, keep in mind the importance of having some early successes. This will build credibility for the plan and create positive momentum and energy amongst employees. As such, some of the first steps should be "quick wins," items that leadership knows are low-risk to implement. Such changes must result in value to the organization, and even if that value is small, it is still positive momentum.

5. **Execute the transformation plan** – As you execute the organization's transformation plan, measure business benefits, and share the results with project team members and then with all employees. Additionally, solicit feedback from front-line employees on the changes they see and whether the changes are improvements from their viewpoints. Also, request their ideas, as the transformation plan needs to be

a living plan, in which the organization adjusts based on lessons learned during execution.

6. **Address organizational culture issues** – The fact that there is a need for significant change indicates issues with organizational culture. As you studied to understand the business and work within the culture, you likely developed views regarding such issues. Referring to the definition of organizational culture, what changes should there be to the organization's shared beliefs and values? And what about the behavior of the organization's leaders? Are they properly communicating and reinforcing revised beliefs and values? If not, can they make the necessary changes to their ongoing communications?

    With initial successes in delivering value via the transformation plan, you are building trust. You can use this trust to begin to shift organizational culture. There must be agreement among the senior leadership team regarding what cultural changes are needed. And recognize that changing organizational culture will take time. Employees will need to see sustained success and value creation from the execution of the transformation plan. With such success comes increasing trust and recognition, as the change is helping both the organization and employees.

7. **Promote the value of the change continuously** – Often, in the throes of implementation, the desired outcomes can get lost in the pressures and details of the change initiative. Many participants lose sight of the value they seek to create. So, routinely pull the team together and discuss where you are in relation to expected outcomes to refresh everyone's commitment to achieving those results. This activity will develop additional trust across the organization and support shifting the organizational culture.

As an example of driving this type of change, when I stepped in as Learning Tree's CEO, it was clear our business model was not sustainable. What had worked in the 1990s, pre-Internet, was not working anymore. While offering instructor-led training on technology topics certainly still had its place, the size of that market was shrinking based on the introduction of on-demand training (Internet-based training you could take whenever you liked). However, the industry also recognized the power of "blended learning," which combines various modes of training, including instructor-led, on-demand, and even on-the-job, to accelerate one's ability to master a subject. When I started with Learning Tree, the company's assets included contracts to provide significant training (sometimes hundreds of courses per year) to some large, internationally-based organizations. So we had an existing client base, along with well-honed processes supported by a number of internally-developed software applications, to serve these customers with instructor-led training.

Ultimately, our transformation plan was to leverage and enhance our processes and software applications to develop a proprietary learning management platform that could support these large organizations in delivering and managing blended learning on a global scale. We could bring a full-service package, providing a scalable managed-service offering, and do so at a cost much less than any organization could do by itself. We could still leverage our real strength in instructor-led training with this approach, but augment our offerings to support a blended learning model. This would differentiate us from other training companies, particularly those offering only on-demand courses.

Luckily, Learning Tree's managers and employees recognized the need for change, including cultural change. So addressing the required cultural change was manageable. With my arrival, we were free to rapidly revamp our shared beliefs and values, to embrace the need to move beyond just instructor-led training to the full suite of blended learning. We also embraced the idea of digital transformation, in which we could become a full-service learning-management provider to large customers.

Being a Change Agent

Serving as a change agent has great potential for your career. But there is considerable downside risk. You must do your homework and assess whether you are the person who can be successful in the change agent role. Do you sufficiently understand the business and the challenges you are to address? Do you have a good understanding of the applicable technology solutions? Do you have credibility in the organization, not because of your position, but based on your knowledge, capability, and respect of your supervisors, peers, and team?

Being a change agent requires not just skills, but ample experience as well. Therefore, it is best to take on a significant change-agent assignment in mid- or later-career. Ideally, a change agent should have lived through at least one organizational transformation. And while every organizational transformation is unique, human nature is uniform. You will see similar obstacles and challenges arise in any change initiative. Your previous experience will help you identify such obstacles early and provide you with approaches to effectively overcome such obstacles.

Conclusion

Being a leader of a meaningful organizational transformation is not only valuable for you, it can also create value for the organization and all of its employees. It can be one of the more meaningful assignments you can have in your career. Yet, it is also one of the more challenging assignments you can undertake, and as such it can have considerable downside risk. While the leverage of new digital technologies enables the re-imagination of business processes, it is rarely the implementation of the technology that is the major risk. Organizational culture, resistance to change, and the need to win over executives and front-line employees to the change are the more significant challenges, and therefore, larger risks. To deal effectively with these risks, you need to have knowledge and experience that builds credibility to lead an organization through such change.

Key Takeaways from Chapter 12: Drive Change

- In today's environment a risk-averse culture can threaten an organization's very existence.

- If you need to drive significant change in your organization, undertake the following steps:

  1. **Understand your business** – You must gain a deep understanding of your organization's business operations.

  2. **Understand and work within the organizational culture** – To build trust, you must honor the positive aspects of the organization's culture.

  3. **Study, adopt, and tailor a specific organizational change management (OCM) methodology** – Pick the one best suited to the situation.

  4. **Develop a transformation plan** – Develop a step-by-step approach to driving the changes in business operations and related IT systems.

  5. **Execute the transformation plan** – As you execute the plan, measure the business benefits and share them with project team members and employees. Solicit feedback from front-line employees.

  6. **Address organizational culture issues** – With initial successes in delivering value via the transformation plan, you build trust. You can use this trust to begin to shift organizational culture.

  7. **Promote the value of the change continuously** – Routinely pull the team together and discuss where you are in relation to expected outcomes.

Being a change agent is one of the more meaningful assignments you can have in your career and can create significant value for you and the organization.

Chapter 13:

Give Back – Help the Next Generation

"If you want to touch the past, touch a rock. If you want to touch the present, touch a flower. If you want to touch the future, touch a life."

Author Unknown

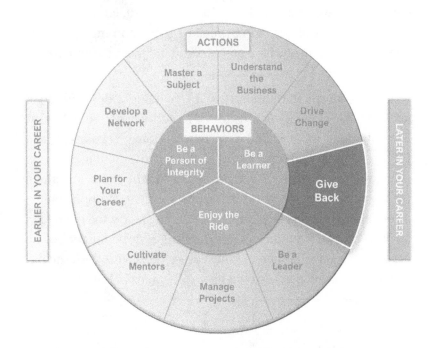

I n the technology field, the support of others is crucial to one's success. Many of us can point to certain bosses or other formal or informal mentors who made such a meaningful difference in our professional lives. A great piece of advice, or the opportunity to step into a leadership role, or support to get us past a particular challenge—these are just some of the ways that others support us in our careers.

Now, one can argue that they put themselves into positions that led to success, and such support from others would have happened, with or without a specific boss's or mentor's actions. Perhaps, but I view it differently. Like my view regarding servant leadership, I have a humble outlook, recognizing that many exceptionally talented individuals I have worked with have supported my development. There have been crucial points in my career in which others, in particular bosses and mentors, have helped me immensely. I am grateful and indebted to them for the trust they placed in me at the time.

Harking back to Chapters 6 and 7, building your professional network and developing a cadre of mentors is so critical. Why? Your mentors' advice can be transformational to your career if you are humble and have the wisdom to accept and incorporate good advice. Further, if you invest in building and sustaining your professional network, it becomes a field of opportunities throughout your career. Ultimately, you must have the good judgment to choose from these opportunities. But the number of opportunities you will have in your career correlates with the size and quality of the professional network you have built.

Giving Back

Given the role that others play in your success, it is logical that you should offer such support to others, particularly later in your career. There is no rule that you must give back, and there are individuals who never feel any compelling need to support others. **But for many, there are significant benefits to helping others in their careers. The benefits can be both emotional and professional.** Emotional benefits include satisfaction and a sense of well-being in providing meaningful support to others. I have found it satisfying to mentor others throughout my career and support their development through advice and teaching moments.

On the professional side, giving back and supporting others to grow in their careers is a leadership trait. As such, being a boss or mentor, and focusing on developing others, enhances your reputation as someone who takes developing talent in your organization seriously. As a supervisor, you can help direct reports by supporting them in developing their KSAs, providing career guidance, and steering them to good opportunities. And this does not just apply to managers or executives. Senior individual contributors, typically those with in-depth technical knowledge in a subject, can become valuable leaders for their organizations. Their leadership is not based on a formal reporting structure but rather on the support and mentorship they offer to others in the organization. These individuals become much more valuable for their organizations, working as force multipliers in others' development.

As you reach mid-career, begin to think about how you can support others. And be sincere in these efforts, both for the emotional and professional benefits. Beyond being a supervisor and supporting your direct reports, you should consider the following ways in which you can give back to others:

1. **Be a mentor to someone, either via a formal program or informally if necessary** – Many mid-and large-sized organizations have formal mentor programs set up to support employees. A formal program is the best way to begin to mentor others, as the organization will work to ensure there is a good match between mentor and mentee. If you

start mid-career, you will be in an excellent position to mentor those just entering the workforce or within the first five years of their careers. These early years are a crucial time for individuals in their careers, and you have the opportunity to meaningfully support them in this formative time.

Even if your organization does not have a formal mentor program, still seek opportunities to mentor. However, it can be awkward within your organization due to how others may view the mentor-mentee relationship. If a mentee is a direct report, be careful, because some may think you are showing favoritism. And be particularly careful in situations in which your mentee is a direct report of one of your peers. A safer approach is to mentor through a professional association (as stated in Chapter 6, you should involve yourself in a professional association). Many associations have formal programs to support mentoring. But whether formal or informal, a mentoring arrangement outside your organization will result in fewer conflicts.

2. **Become an advisor** – Being a mentor is a personal one-on-one relationship you develop with another individual to support their career development. Another way to support others is to become an advisor, typically to a small group or project team. While you may offer and become an advisor to teams within your organization, you also can look outside your organization. Professional associations almost always have ongoing projects related to improving various aspects of technology or process disciplines. Early in your career, you should get involved in some of these projects to further your expertise, build your professional network, and identify mentors. Later in your career, you can advise such teams, sharing your expertise in a subject and ensuring the project team focuses on delivering value that can be useful for all in your profession.

As an example, I have played an advisory role within the American Council for Technology – Industry Advisory Council (ACT-IAC), whose mission is to support improving government through the use of technology. Within ACT-IAC, there are currently eight communities of interest (COIs), including areas as diverse as emerging technology, customer experience, and cybersecurity. Given my experience and expertise in IT management, I have been a senior advisor over the past five years to the IT Management and Modernization COI, which focuses on projects to advance government agencies' capabilities to better manage and modernize their IT. I have found this to be an excellent way to give back, offering the chance to make a broad impact in an area that I am passionate about improving.

3. **Teach in your area of expertise** – If you have developed expertise in a subject of technology or a related process discipline, you may wish to use this expertise to teach. You may think about teaching courses at a college level, and if you aspire to do so, that is wonderful. But you can try teaching short courses related to your expertise first, perhaps just for those in your organization, or maybe for a training company. I was surprised at the number of instructors we had at Learning Tree who worked full-time but still wanted to teach. These individuals would usually teach a three- or four-day course a couple of times a year.

When I was at Learning Tree, I co-authored three courses and had the opportunity to teach each one of them on a relatively infrequent basis. I came to enjoy these teaching assignments. Not only was it heartening to see individuals expand their understanding of a particular subject, but I found it helped me keep current on the subject. Furthermore, some of the attendees would provide me new insights based on their experiences.

You should not expect to do all of these activities simultaneously. Yet, it is likely that as you continue to have more success in your career, you will have additional opportunities and means to give back.

Conclusion

There is no rule regarding how you should support others. It is a highly personal decision, and other aspects of your professional and personal life determine how much time you can dedicate to supporting others. Indeed, you should put your family and career first. But as you move into mid-career and certainly later in your career, you should think about how you can incorporate activities in your career plan that focus on others' development. Perhaps you can only mentor one or two individuals during mid-career, or do a little teaching. It is likely that once you start, it becomes more important in your career planning. There is a sense of accomplishment and serenity that comes with doing good for others. And there is hardly anything more important than helping others grow, so they are more likely to reach their career goals.

Key Takeaways from Chapter 13: Give Back

- In the technology field, the support of others is crucial to one's success.

- For many of us, there are significant benefits to helping others in their careers. The benefits can be emotional as well as professional.

- Emotionally, giving back provides satisfaction and a sense of well-being. It is satisfying to mentor others and support their development through advice and teaching moments.

- Professionally, giving back and supporting others to grow in their careers is a leadership trait. As such, being a boss or mentor, and focusing on developing others, enhances your reputation as someone who takes developing talent in your organization seriously.

- As you reach mid-career, begin to think about how you can support others. In particular, consider the following ways in which you can give back:

  1. **Be a mentor to someone, either via a formal program or informally if necessary** – Look to mentor someone in your organization if you have a formal program, or consider mentoring through a professional association you are involved in.

  2. **Become an advisor** – Become an advisor, typically to a small group or project team. While you may offer and become an advisor to teams within your organization, also look outside your organization, perhaps through a professional association.

  3. **Teach in your area of expertise** – A meaningful way to give back is to teach. If you have developed expertise in an area of technology or a related process discipline, you may wish to use this expertise as a teacher. This can be at a college level, internal to your organization, or via a training company focused on technology-based subjects.

There is a sense of accomplishment and serenity that comes with doing good for others. And there is hardly anything more important than helping others grow, so they are more likely to reach their career goals.

Chapter 14:

In Closing

"Success is not the key to happiness. Happiness is the key to success. If you love what you are doing, you will be successful."

Albert Schweitzer

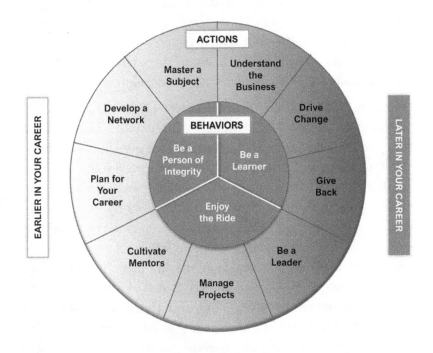

This book encompasses twelve recommendations that can support you in a career in the technology field. Three of these recommendations address necessary behaviors you should adopt and live by throughout your career. Nine recommendations are actions, some of which are more likely to occur and be of higher value to you earlier in your career—some later in your career.

One of the most important recommendations is to develop and maintain a career plan (as described in Chapter 5). This career plan should contain your long-term career goals and an analysis that describes the competencies (KSAs and behaviors) you will need to develop to reach those goals. Your plan should also include a career path plan that describes the positions you plan to hold and the experiences you hope to gain along your career journey. Furthermore, your career plan should include an individual development plan (IDP), containing specific actions you will be taking over the next five years to develop your KSAs.

In reflecting on this level of career planning, you may be thinking it is not realistic. You may think that there are just too many unknowns as you look ahead two or even three decades, and that attempting to plan that far in advance is futile. You may think that, whatever your plan, there will be setbacks that throw you off your path, or there will be unforeseen opportunities that lead you to a new path. So, in the face of such uncertainty, why should you undertake such a planning effort? And why should you follow the other recommendations in this book and include them in your planning? The answer is that regardless of what happens in the future, **preparing and then executing your plan will accelerate the development of the competencies to move you toward your career goals.** It also gives you a yardstick to measure your levels of achievement, as well as a baseline with which to evaluate emerging opportunities and address challenges. If, at some future point, you decide to change your plan and set different career goals, you will be doing so with greater capabilities, along with the self-awareness of what you want out of your career.

Self-Awareness

Let's return to the topic of self-awareness. While the twelve recommendations in this book are concrete and action-oriented, self-awareness, while critically important to long-term career success, is hard to address directly. **How does one become more self-aware? In terms of your career, the answer is to cultivate a set of mentors who can provide you appropriate feedback, supporting you in developing that vital understanding of yourself.** Ultimately, if you want success in your career, you will need to play to your innate strengths and compensate for your weaknesses.

To make this concept tangible, I will use myself as an example. As described earlier in this book, I have a passion for improving how our government operates, having spent more than eight years in the U.S. federal government and also having served as a contractor to government agencies. For the past twenty years or so, I have thought that it would be wonderful to be an elected official, in which I could have even more impact, perhaps in a state or federal legislature. Yet, when I look at what it takes to run for elective office, I am realistic that my capabilities are not well suited to running for an elective office. It does not mean I have fewer capabilities than others, but rather that my capabilities are different than what you will find in almost all politicians.

I circle back to this issue of self-awareness because it is so essential to your career. You may be incredibly passionate regarding a particular career path you wish to take. But if you do not have the innate capabilities to add significant value in your work, you will never achieve your career goals. As I previously stressed, you need good mentors early in your career—individuals you respect who can provide you constructive feedback, some of which might be quite difficult for you to hear. Early in your career, with good mentors and the proper self-awareness, you can focus on finding a career path that is right for you.

Persistence

Another trait that is relevant to you in your career is persistence. President Calvin Coolidge's quote sums it up nicely:

> *"Nothing in this world will take the place of persistence. Talent will not; nothing is more common than unsuccessful men with talent. Genius will not; unrewarded genius is almost a proverb. Education will not; the world is full of educated derelicts. Persistence and determination alone are omnipotent."*

It is easy to state "have persistence" as a recommendation. But does it make sense to have persistence if the actual probability of you being successful in that endeavor is exceptionally low? And can you persist in the work if you have not developed a passion for what you are doing?

Back in 2006, I invested in a start-up company in the financial services industry. I have little background in commercial financial services, but one of the two founders is a friend. He had been highly successful working for others in the financial services industry, had a groundbreaking idea, and as he described his vision, his passion was palpable. He had also brought on a partner, a person who was an excellent complement to my friend, both in capabilities and demeanor. I decided to invest, but only because of the capabilities and passion of the founders. They then asked me to join the board of directors, which I was pleased to do.

Unluckily, the financial crisis of 2008 hit soon after they had begun offering their first products. This company then struggled for the next seven years, facing economic headwinds to win new customers and build a brand. The two founders maintained their enthusiasm through that low period, continued to innovate, and showed remarkable persistence. Now, in 2021, their business is thriving—growing rapidly and proving to be quite profitable. I am so pleased for these founders, as their persistence enabled their success. But their persistence was based on their collective capabilities, along with their passion for making the idea a reality.

So, with your mentors' help, make sure you understand yourself and that your innate skills and abilities line up with your career goals. And make sure those career goals are something that you are passionate about, something that gives you great satisfaction in knowing that your success will not just be good for yourself, but also for others. **Once you align your skills and abilities with career goals that you are passionate about, you will undoubtedly have the persistence to see yourself to success.** The recommendations, particularly related to developing a career plan, cultivating mentors, and enjoying the ride, are meant to put you in the best position to find that alignment for you.

Patience

Lastly, related to persistence is the trait of patience. Persistence is defined as "firm continuance in a course of action in spite of difficulty or opposition," while patience is "the capacity to accept or tolerate delay, trouble, or suffering without getting angry or upset." The recommendations in this book challenge you to plan, developing a written career plan with goals and objectives and an IDP for the next five years to foster your professional development. But few milestones in life are achieved as quickly as we would like. This will undoubtedly be the case with a number of the career milestones you set. Accepting such delays as a given will help soften the blow when things don't go your way.

And think of such delays as opportunities. Perhaps you won't land that first project manager assignment as soon as you had planned. Use that additional time to learn more, gaining more experience working on projects—when the opportunity arrives, you will be even more prepared to handle it well and be successful. **Being patient does not mean giving up on being proactive, on having persistence.**

Conclusion

There are many types of positions and career paths you can take in the technology field. My ideal career, while right for me, is certainly not right for you. You need to decide on your career goals, put in place the plans, and take the actions to move you toward those goals. But most importantly, strive to find a career in which you have a passion for the work. Having a career in which you love your work, your work is meaningful to you and others, and you do your work with integrity is, in and of itself, success.

Key Takeaways from Chapter 14: In Closing

- This book encompasses twelve recommendations that can support you in a career in the technology field. Three of these recommendations address necessary behaviors you should adopt and live by throughout your career. Nine recommendations are actions that support you throughout your career.

- Developing and then executing your career plan and associated IDP will increase your skills, experience, and self-awareness. You will be making sustained progress toward a set of meaningful career goals. If you decide to set different career goals at some point, then you will have done so with greater capabilities, along with the self-awareness of what you want out of your career.

- Self-awareness, while critically important to long-term career success, is hard to address directly. Cultivate a set of mentors who can provide you appropriate feedback, supporting you in developing that vital understanding of yourself. Ultimately, if you want success in your career, you will need to play to your innate strengths and compensate for your weaknesses.

- Persistence is an essential career trait that is also hard to address directly. Once you align your skills and abilities with a career goal that you are passionate about, you will undoubtedly have the persistence to see yourself to success.

- You will achieve few career milestones in life as quickly as you would like. Have patience, and think of such delays as opportunities for further development.

- You need to decide on your career goals, put in place the plans, and take the actions to move you toward those goals. But through all of this, strive to find a career in which you have a passion for the work.

Having a career in which you love your work, your work is meaningful to you and others, and you do your work with integrity is, in and of itself, success.

Acknowledgments

First, I am grateful to have had the privilege to work with so many dedicated professionals throughout my career. I have learned much from so many excellent people who have been mentors and colleagues.

I asked several individuals who have been successful in the technology field to review my manuscript and provide me feedback for consideration, including:

- Melvin Brown II – Melvin has had a distinguished career in IT in the U.S. civilian federal government after starting his career in the U.S. Marine Corp. He currently serves as an executive in the U.S. Office of Personnel Management (OPM). I enjoyed working with Melvin at the DHS when he was successfully managing some critical DHS IT programs, including the Homeland Security Information Network (HSIN).

- Erica Elam – Erica is a noted trainer, coach, and instructional designer in agility and innovation, conscious leadership, and IT. I met Erica when I was at Learning Tree International, and I have always admired her teaching style, notably her ability to integrate leadership, management, and technology disciplines.

- Magnus Nylund – Magnus has spent his career at Learning Tree International, starting as a software developer and rising to become CIO of the company when I joined as CEO. Magnus impressed me not only with his technical and management capabilities, but also his understanding of Learning Tree's business. After working with Magnus for a year, I asked him to become Learning Tree's chief operating officer (COO), the position he currently holds.

- John Reece – John has had an illustrious career in technology, including serving as a technologist, project/program manager, partner at Booz, Allen & Hamilton, and the CIO at Time Warner as well as the IRS. I first met John when I joined the IRS, and sought him out given his past work there. I worked closely with John when I was DHS CIO and he was consulting for DHS headquarters and several of the DHS components.

- Robert Shay – Bob has had a distinguished career in the IT professional services field, rising to become a partner at Ernst & Young and the COO of Capgemini Government Solutions after they acquired E&Y's consulting business. I met Bob when I was consulting for Capgemini and found him one of the more insightful IT leaders with whom I have worked.

- Renee Wynn – Renee recently retired from government service, with her last assignment serving as the NASA CIO. Renee and I got to know each other well when she served as president of the American Council for Technology (ACT), and I was chairman of the sister organization, the Industry Advisory Council (IAC). Renee is an excellent technology manager, but more importantly, a passionate and highly effective leader.

I thank each of these individuals for their feedback—this book is much improved because of their suggestions.

I want to thank my editor, Sue Mellen, who helped turn my draft prose into a book of which I am proud. Thanks to Doreen La Velle, who took my ideas and developed professional-quality graphics for the book. Thanks to Rob Hudgins for his creativity in designing the book's cover and the internal book layout quality. And thanks to Angela Hoy and the team at the publisher, Book-Locker.com, Inc., who helped me, as a first-time book author, through the publishing process.

Finally, on a personal note, I would like to thank my wife, Jackie. She has always encouraged and supported me throughout my career, and she has been a wonderful partner and mentor.

Suggested Additional Reading

A s described in this book, the technology field is now quite diverse, with thousands of distinct roles. Given how quickly technologies and process disciplines evolve, any reading list containing books on technologies or process disciplines would soon be out of date.

The following list of books addresses vital topics related to professional human interactions and organization, such as leadership, management, and organizational change management. It is by no means an exhaustive list, but meant to support you as starting points on your journey of developing KSAs in the "power skills" for dealing with people.

Personal Development
Emotional Intelligence: Why It Can Matter More than IQ, Daniel Goleman

Finding Your Own North Star: Claiming the Life You Were Meant to Live, Martha Beck

The 7 Habits of Highly Effective People: Powerful Lessons in Personal Change, Stephen R. Covey

The Power of Habit: Why We Do What We Do in Life and Business, Charles Duhigg

Leadership
Leaders Eat Last, Simon Sinek

Leadership is an Art, Max DePree

The Five Dysfunctions of a Team: A Leadership Fable, Patrick Lencioni

The Hard Thing about Hard Things: Building a Business When There Are No Easy Answers, Ben Horowitz

Change Management

Good to Great: Why Some Companies Make the Leap…and Others Don't, Jim Collins

Leading Change, John Kotter

Measure What Matters: How Google, Bono, and the Gates Foundation Rock the World with OKRs, John Doerr

The Speed of Trust: The One Thing That Changes Everything, Stephen M. R. Covey

Index

About the Author

Richard A. Spires' background features leadership positions in both the public and private sectors. Besides serving as CIO at both the IRS and U.S. Department of Homeland Security, he served in several leadership roles in the private sector, including president of Mantas, Inc. and CEO and a director of Learning Tree International. During his tenure at the IRS, he led the Business Systems Modernization (BSM) program, one of the largest technology modernization programs ever undertaken and that has served as a blueprint for organizational transformation. A theme that has run through his career has been using advanced technologies and operational systems to transform the way organizations function.

Richard is currently an independent consultant providing advice to companies and government agencies in strategy, digital transformation, operations, and business development. He also currently serves on the Board of Directors of MAXIMUS Federal, a leading federal system integrator, and RateReset Corporation, a leading provider of loan reset products serving the banking and credit union industries. He also serves on the Palo Alto Networks Public Sector Advisory Council, MetroStar Systems Advisory Board, and he recently served as the chairman of the board of ACT-IAC, a leading non-profit organization serving government IT.

Richard has won numerous awards for his leadership in IT, including the 2020 ACT-IAC Industry Executive Leadership Award, 2012 Fed 100 Government Executive Eagle Award, TechAmerica's 2012 Government Executive of the Year, and Government Computer News 2011 Civilian Government Executive of the Year. He was inducted into The George Washington University Engineering Hall of Fame in 2019 and named a Distinguished Alumnus of the University of Cincinnati's College of Engineering in 2006.

Richard received a B.S. in Electrical Engineering and a B.A. in Mathematical Sciences from the University of Cincinnati. He also holds an M.S. in Electrical Engineering from The George Washington University.

Richard lives in Virginia with his wife, Jackie. They have three adult children.